Managing telework

To Olga, my Mother, my Father
and my Grandfather, who died shortly before this book was completed

To Kerry, Fiona and Luke for living the experience of 'spillover'

To Kerry, Kira and Sean for giving me the best possible reason for teleworking

Managing telework

Edited by
Kevin Daniels
David Lamond
Peter Standen

Business Press
Thomson Learning™

Australia • Canada • Denmark • Japan • Mexico • New Zealand • Philippines
Puerto Rico • Singapore • South Africa • Spain • United Kingdom • United States

Managing Telework

Business Press is a division of Thomson Learning. The Thomson Learning logo is a registered trademark used herein under licence.

For more information, contact Business Press, Berkshire House, 168–173 High Holborn, London, WC1V 7AA or visit us on the World Wide Web at: http: //www.itbp.com.

British Library Cataloguing-in-Publication Data
A catalogue record for this book is available from the British Library

ISBN 1–86152–572–9

First edition published 2000 by Thomson Learning

Typeset by Saxon Graphics
Printed in Singapore by Kin Keong

List of contributors

John Allan   Institute of Educational Technology, Open University, UK

Jon Billsberry   Open University Business School, UK

Ken Giles   Open University Business School, UK

Richard Harper   Digital World Research Centre, University of Surrey, UK

Jean Marie Hiltrop   Department of Management, University of Otago, New Zealand

Maryam Omari   School of Management, Edith Cowan University, Australia

Jos van Ommeren   School of Management, Cranfield University

Gilly Salmon   Open University Business School, UK

Paul Sparrow   School of Management, University of Sheffield, UK

Olga Tregaskis   School of Business, de Montfort University, UK

Kevin Daniels is Reader in Organizational Behaviour at Sheffield University Management School, UK. He has a PhD in applied psychology and is a Chartered Psychologist. He researches teleworking and the links between organizations, cognition and psychological well-being. He has worked with many large private and public sector organizations on developing psychologically healthy work environments and the human resource management of teleworkers.

David Lamond is a registered psychologist, and Senior Lecturer in Management and Director of Special Projects for the Macquarie Graduate School of Management (MGSM), at Macquarie University in Sydney, Australia. David joined MGSM in 1990, following a successful career as a senior public sector manager, working in local and State government in New South Wales. David's research interests focus on three areas – the psychology of managerial behaviour; teleworking as a new form of work; and the history of management thought and management pedagogy. He also consults extensively both locally and internationally.

Peter Standen is a Senior Lecturer in the School of Management at Edith Cowan University in Perth, Australia. He has a PhD in psychology from the University of Western Australia, and has authored a number of papers based on large-scale research projects on telework in Australia. Current research interests include the well-being of teleworkers, their management, and more generally the role of information and communications technology in delocalizing work. Peter consults on telework in Western Australia.

Contents

Preface

This is a book about teleworking by three teleworkers, two of whom have never met each other face-to-face. Kevin and David met in 1994, while David was on sabbatical in the UK, and a firm friendship was formed, with talk of 'doing some work together'. In 1996, while David was carrying out his role as Associate Editor of the *Journal of the Australian and New Zealand Academy of Management*, he sent an excited e-mail to Kevin, saying he'd just finished reading an article on teleworking submitted for the journal, and 'this fellow can write'. Peter was contacted by e-mail, and agreed to be involved. The aim was to produce a paper outlining the major issues in the human resource management of teleworking. Several papers later, we continue to work together, with various other projects in the pipeline, but still only on a teleworking basis (David and Peter met for the first and only time 5 minutes before they were due to deliver one of these papers, at a conference in Sydney, in 1997; Kevin and Peter have never met).

Managing Telework is our most ambitious project and, we believe, our most valuable contribution to date. In this book, we aim to provide a basis for more informed management practice in this area by gathering and integrating in one volume current thinking on different aspects of telework. We hope that the book will give practitioners and students a clear, concise and comprehensive view of the area. Throughout the book, we aim to keep a firm focus on using knowledge and theory to enhance practice in this area.

As you read the book, you may care to recall how it was developed – by many of the same teleworking processes that are discussed. Meanwhile we look forward to the day when we three will all meet together for the first time.

KD, Sheffield, DL, Sydney, PS, Perth
June 1999

Chapter 1

Managing telework: an introduction to the issues

Kevin Daniels, David Lamond and Peter Standen

In this opening chapter, we outline the key issues managers must address if they are to manage teleworkers effectively. By examining the salient issues, we develop a framework for understanding telework. In essence, the framework provides a basis for the rest of the chapters in this book. The approach we take in this book is unashamedly behavioural. This is not to say other approaches are not important – not least the technology that enables telework or the taxation issues that surround telework (see e.g. Gray *et al.*, 1993). We take this approach because the management of teleworkers, *as a human process*, means understanding the social and organizational context of telework, and modifying management systems and approaches to match these contexts. Before we move on to describing our framework and introducing the rest of the chapters in the book, we examine why telework has become so popular and define what we mean by telework.

An introduction to telework

From the days when it was described as the 'next workplace revolution' (Kelly, 1985), interest in teleworking has grown among workers, employers, transportation planners, communities, the telecommunications industry, and others (Handy and Mokhtarian, 1996). Telework is set to increase in the future. Huws (1993) found that 6 per cent of her sample of 1000 UK employers already employed teleworkers, and a further 8 per cent expected to introduce teleworking. In the United States, in a survey of 305 senior US executives, 70 per cent predicted that teleworking would increase in their companies throughout 1996 (Frazee, 1996).

There are many reasons to expect organizations and their employees to experiment with telework, particularly given the rapid growth of affordable telecommunications technology. Indeed, the list of potential benefits is impressive, but there are also many possible negative consequences of teleworking. Table 1.1 shows the advantages and disadvantages listed in the literature.

TABLE 1.1   Possible advantages and disadvantages of telework

	Advantages	Disadvantages

Organizational	Lower accommodation costs
	Better recruitment and
	    retention
	Increased productivity
	Resilience to extreme
	    conditions (e.g. weather)
		Increased selection, training support costs
		Difficulties supervizing and motivating
		Socializing new employees
		Difficulties with planning/performance
		    measures

Individual	Flexibility
	More time for home and
	    family
	Reduced commuting
	Job autonomy
	Less disturbance whilst
	    working
	Chance to remain in work
	    despite moving home
		Fewer opportunities for development or
		    promotion
		Conflict between work and home
		Lower job security
		Social isolation
		More time spent working
		Routinization of tasks
		Teleworkers perceive themselves as
		    valued less

Societal	Increased community
	    stability
	Increased entrepreneurial
	    activity
	Less pollution
	More efficient use of energy	

Source: Lamond *et al.* (1997)

Without a systematic framework, it is difficult to assess how one can realize the benefits of teleworking without encountering the pitfalls. Before we can develop such a framework, however, we must be clear exactly what we mean by telework. Telework is a multifaceted phenomenon (Lamond *et al.*, 1997). Two of the central components involve working from non-traditional locations and using information and computer technology (Gray *et al.*, 1993). The information technology can vary in sophistication from simply using a telephone to arrangements with faxes, modems and e-mail links. We can also distinguish amongst different locations where teleworkers can operate for more or less of the time (e.g. Gray *et al.*, 1993; Huws, 1994):

- *home-based telework* where work duties are carried out at home;
- *teleworking from remote offices* where work is done at offices that are remote from the main office – at 'satellite offices' (controlled by the employer); at telecentres (information technology and workspace is provided for a given community and employers are asked to rent space for their employees); or at telecottages (where training is provided for users, and attempts are made to attract employment for self-employed teleworkers);
- *mobile telework*: where work is done by people who usually spend a great deal of time travelling and/or on customers' premises (e.g. sales, consulting).

Telework is much broader than just alternative locations for work supported by information technology. For example, Olsen (1989) has made the distinction between telework that is 'professional, managerial or technical' and telework that is 'clerical, manufacturing or semi-skilled'. There are some differences between high and low knowledge intensity work relevant to managing teleworkers (Leidner, 1988). High knowledge intensity jobs have outputs which are not easily measured and involve greater autonomy over work conditions. Low knowledge intensity work involves work that is more routine, outputs that are more easily measured and less autonomy.

Another important aspect of telework is the degree of communication between the teleworker and others. One aspect of this is communication with other members of the organization. This reflects the nature of the employment relationship (employee/consultant) and the degree of 'embeddedness' within the organization (e.g. level of responsibility and necessary contact with other members of the organization). For some teleworkers (e.g. mobile teleworkers, telesales), communication with people external to the organization is an important part of work. For others (e.g. home-based programmers), there is hardly any external contact.

We consider it important to examine teleworking as a bundle of practices that vary across five dimensions (Lamond *et al.*, 1997):

> *Dimension 1 – IT usage:* extent of use of telecommunications/IT links – home/mobile computer, fax, modem, phone, mobile phone, use of WWW sites;
> *Dimension 2 – knowledge intensity:* extent of knowledge required, ease of output measures and autonomy of work;
> *Dimension 3 – intra-organizational contact*: extent of communication with other people in the organization;
> *Dimension 4 – extra-organizational contact*: extent of communication with people outside the organization;
> *Dimension 5 – location:* the amount of time spent in the different locations: traditional office, home, remote office/telecottage, mobile.

This approach has the advantage of offering a more fine-grained approach to telework that is able to distinguish amongst the extent to which people engage in different teleworking practices, and consequently provides a better platform for choosing appropriate management styles and systems for different teleworkers. Table 1.2 shows how using such dimensions can classify different jobs.

A framework for managing teleworkers

Teleworking exists at the juncture of a variety of organizational, social and individual characteristics and processes. In this section, we outline a comprehensive framework that shows how these forces are connected (Lamond *et al.*, 1997). Figure 1.1 shows this framework. The framework highlights three major components of managing teleworkers: matching telework to the wider organizational context; issues in managing individual teleworkers; and matching telework with management systems. These three components correspond to the three remaining parts of this book.

TABLE 1.2 Classifying teleworkers

	High knowledge intensity				Low knowledge intensity			
	Intra-organizational contact High		Low		Intra-organizational contact High		Low	
	External contact High	Low	External contact High	Low	External contact High	Low	External contact High	Low
Home-based	Sales managers	Accountant Programmer	Lawyer	IS developer Architect	Customer inquiries Phone operator	Secretarial/ Clerical	Phone sales	Clerical Data entry
Remote office	Sales managers	Programmer	Lawyer	IS developer	Customer inquiries Phone operator	Secretarial/ Clerical	Phone sales	Clerical Data entry
Mobile	Sales managers Engineers	Internal consultants	Community nurse Assessor	IS developer	Service persons	Secretarial/ Clerical	Sales representative Delivery staff	Clerical Data entry

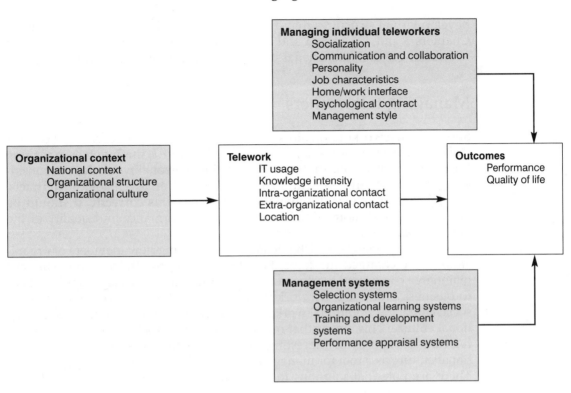

FIGURE 1.1   A framework for managing telework

Telework and the organizational context

Choosing whether to implement a teleworking programme means assessing the likely match of telework to the organizational environment. This entails assessing the congruence of different teleworking practices with existing systems and cultures, whether at the level of the organization or at the national level. The purpose of the chapters in the first section of this book is to explore the contingencies of an organization's environment that encourage effective teleworking.

Telework is more common in some countries than others. In Europe, for example, there are important differences amongst its constituent countries from north to south, with less teleworking generally in the southern countries. Such differences could be due to many factors, including changing labour force characteristics, legislation and changes in societal attitudes. In Chapter 2, Tregaskis explores these issues. Contemporary changes in organizational structures and cultures might also encourage teleworking. These changes include downsizing, delayering, process re-engineering, project-based structures, the shift to a core/periphery model (with a greater role for contingent workers), and growth in inter-organizational networks. The growth of knowledge work and the increased sophistication of information technology make it easier to develop virtual structures that transcend traditional space and time limits. In Chapters 3 and 4, Lamond and Standen examine the relationships between teleworking and organizational structures and cultures respectively.

Managing teleworkers

Successful teleworking requires examining the group and individual context and managing it as necessary. As shown in Figure 1.1, this involves managing the processes of socialization, communication, personality, job design, considering the home environment, managing implicit or psychological contracts, and line management. By managing these systems correctly, it should be possible to build motivation, commitment, performance and quality of life amongst teleworkers.

Social relationships, which encompass socializing new members of organizations, are changed fundamentally by teleworking. Indeed, to create and maintain a committed workforce, it is important to link socialization practices to business processes. Teleworkers do not have the same opportunities for social contact as traditional workers and are not as immersed in the organizational culture. This means that many of the usual socialization factors are not relevant. This poses an interesting paradox as managers seek to use organizational culture as a tool for management control in place of direct supervision. There are potential solutions to this paradox, which Billsberry describes in Chapter 5. Communication and decision making are also important parts of the social processes of teleworking. Face-to-face communication is likely to be highest between managers and traditional workers, and lowest between managers and teleworkers. Full use of information technology could overcome some barriers, as would regular meetings that involve all workers. Nevertheless, some problems of communicating and collaborating at a distance will remain. In Chapter 6, Harper presents a case study of how technology is adapted to enable communication and collaboration at a distance, and highlights a method to help ensure the best implementation and use of information technology within specific organizational contexts.

Arguably, individual factors become prominent in the success of teleworking – where the influence of group norms can be diminished. Indeed, personality is an important influence on behaviour in more traditional work arrangements. In Chapter 7, Lamond considers personality in the context of teleworking. Recognizing that there are many different forms of teleworking, he argues that it is necessary to ensure that an individual's personality is matched to the characteristics of the teleworking to be performed. This has clear implications for selecting teleworkers.

We also expect the job characteristics of different teleworkers to be different from other workers. These differences have implications for the well-being of teleworkers, as well as their overall motivation. There are conflicting arguments on the implications of telework for health. Some writers speculate that teleworking practices increase autonomy over work and free up time for non-work activities – enhancing job and life satisfaction. Critics argue that teleworking practices decrease autonomy, increase demands and reduce the time for non-work activities as traditional spatial boundaries between work and home are erased. In Chapter 8, Daniels reviews the effects of teleworking practices on work-related health, and the strategies that can be used to ensure healthy job design. Standen continues along this route in Chapter 9. In particular, he examines the joint effects of home-based teleworking and the home environment on psychological health, and the strategies for ensuring congruence between work and non-work life.

However, even where personality, job design and home environments are conducive to teleworking, other individual problems might surface stemming from violations of the psychological contract, as highlighted by Sparrow in Chapter 10. Sparrow considers how teleworking can alter psychological contracting, and how, without careful attention, teleworking can become a low-trust work arrangement. Managers can certainly help avoid the problems outlined by Sparrow, and in Chapter 11, Lamond considers some of the approaches to managing teleworkers. It becomes clear that there is no easy, nor one best, way to manage teleworkers. Rather, and perhaps not surprisingly, it is the case that many of the principles of good management are as applicable to teleworking as they are to traditional work arrangements.

Human resource management systems

In the previous section, we discussed the issues highlighted in Figure 1.1, and considered how these may be managed at the operational or tactical level of the organization. Many of the principles of good telework management at an individual level need to be supported by wider organizational systems if the organizational objectives of teleworking are to be realized. Selection, performance management, training and development systems are all important in this regard.

In Chapter 12, Omari and Standen bring together material from earlier chapters on personality, socialization, organizational culture, and well-being with their own research to inform a systemic approach to selecting teleworkers. Chapters 13 and 14 highlight the importance of developing human resources to ensure performance, learning and innovation. Like Omari and Standen, Tregaskis and Daniels draw on earlier chapters as well as other sources to argue in Chapter 13 for a broad and participative approach to organizational learning for teleworkers that spans organizational, managerial and technical boundaries. In Chapter 14, Salmon *et al.* examine training and development at a distance in more detail. Using a case study of their own experiences in this area, they illustrate many important principles, not just for delivering training using new media, but also for embedding that training within the wider social system. In Chapter 15, Van Ommeren examines performance management from an economic perspective. Using a strong theoretical framework, he shows how current teleworking practices in this area might be ineffective in many circumstances, but also how performance can be encouraged even in low-trust environments.

Conclusion

So far in this chapter, we have presented a framework that outlines the major challenges to managing teleworkers. Figure 1.1 summarizes the challenges within the framework, and is a useful tool to help focus on the issues managers need to address before implementing telework schemes. Yet implementing teleworking schemes also requires change management skills, and will often require managers to become teleworkers themselves. In Chapter 16, Hiltrop examines such issues within the broad context of strategic human resource management systems. He outlines the challenges organizations will face and the skills managers must develop to achieve the maximum benefits from teleworking. In the final chapter, we draw together the chapters of this book to show the importance of viewing telework through multiple lenses. This enables the management of a multitude of processes in ways sensitive to the inherent variety of both teleworking practices and the people engaged in teleworking, and highlights the need to integrate teleworking practices within the wider strategic and social context of the organization for the benefit of teleworkers and the organization.

In the rest of the book, as we have outlined, each chapter introduces specific advice for a comprehensive, yet detailed approach to managing telework.

References

Frazee, V. (1996) Support for telecommuting is on the rise. *Personnel Journal*, **75**, 22.

Gray, M., Hodson, N. and Gordon, G. (1993) *Teleworking Explained*. Chichester: Wiley.

Handy, S.L. and Mokhtarian, P.L. (1996) The future of telecommuting. *Futures*, **28**, 227–40.

Huws, U. (1993) *Teleworking in Britain: A Report to the Employment Department*. London: Employment Department Research Series.

Huws, U. (1994) *Teleworking*. Brussels: European Commission's Employment Task Force (Directorate General V).

Kelly, M.M. (1985) The next workplace revolution: telecommuting. *Supervisory Management*, **30**, 2–7.

Lamond, D.A., Daniels, K. and Standen, P. (1997) Virtual working or working virtually? An overview of contextual and behavioural issues in teleworking. *Proceedings of the Fourth International Meeting of the Decision Sciences Institute*, Part II, 477–81.

Leidner, R. (1988) Homework: A study in the interaction of work and family organization. *Research in the Sociology of Work*, **4**, 69–94.

Olsen, M.H. (1989) Work at home for computer professionals: current attitudes and future prospects. *ACM Transaction on Office Information Systems*, **7**, 317–38.

Chapter 2

Telework in its national context

Olga Tregaskis

The wide array of definitions used to describe teleworking makes it extremely difficult to gauge the extent of growth and adoption of this form of flexible working by employers and individuals. Nevertheless, anecdotal evidence clearly indicates that employers cannot afford to ignore teleworking as a viable flexible employment option, from both the points of view of employee and business demands for flexibility and adaptability. Equally, technological advances make teleworking not only theoretically possible but also financially affordable. It is not the aim of this chapter to discuss the management of teleworking systems, as these are covered elsewhere in the book. Rather, we will compare the macro labour market conditions within countries that provide the backcloth for organizational practice. We will look at how differences in national approaches to teleworking act to support or hinder the introduction of and demand for teleworking. We will begin by taking a look at what the statistics say on the extent of teleworking.

Extent of teleworking: international comparisons

Figures published by the European Commission (1998) suggest that the number of individuals involved in telework within Europe varies between 1.1 million and 4 million depending on the definition of telework applied. For example, using a broader definition, the European Commission (1998) estimates that teleworking has risen from approximately 2 million in 1997 to around 4 million (3.1 per cent of the European workforce) in mid-1998. This broad definition of teleworking includes:

- people employed on corporate teleworking schemes;
- people working from home with the personal agreement of their line manager but not part of a formal corporate teleworking scheme;
- self-employed who work from home;
- field workers who use their home as a base;
- customer service staff who work in centralized telecommunications-based teams.

The lower estimate of 1.1 million or 0.8 per cent of the European workforce is based on a classification that includes only those people who are part of a formal corporate teleworking scheme. The discrepancy between the two estimates clearly demonstrates definitional ambiguity. This makes it difficult for policy makers to gauge the significance of teleworking on the profile of the labour market and the consequences for social security and employment law provision.

The level of teleworking varies considerable across countries. Table 2.1 shows the estimates for the percentage of the workforce in 13 European countries involved in teleworking. These estimates are based on the broad definition of teleworking discussed above. According to these figures Denmark (9.7 per cent of the workforce), the Netherlands (9.1 per cent of the workforce) and the UK (7.0 per cent of the workforce) are the top three European users of this mode of work. Finland, Ireland, Sweden and Belgium have between 5.3 per cent and 6.3 per cent of their total workforce teleworking. The use of teleworking in the remaining northern and southern European countries falls dramatically, ranging from 1.9 per cent of the German workforce to as low as 0.6 per cent in Spain.

Comparing teleworking levels becomes more difficult when we look beyond Europe as, once again, different definitions are in use. Despite this,

TABLE 2.1   Estimates of teleworking*, population density and urbanization, 1997

Country	Number of teleworkers (000)	% of the total workforce teleworking	Population density – persons per sq. km	Urbanization – % of the total population
Denmark	250	9.7	122.4	85
Netherlands	600	9.1	379.1	89
UK	1,800	7.0	239.5	89
Finland	150	6.3	15.3	64
Ireland	50	6.1	52.3	58
Sweden	180	5.4	19.7	83
Belgium	200	5.3	332.5	97
Germany	600	1.9	229.6	87
Austria	50	1.5	96.6	64
Portugal	60	1.3	108.4	37
France	240	1.1	107.7	75
Italy	180	0.9	190.6	67
Spain	80	0.6	77.9	77
Greece	Nc	Nc	79.7	60
Luxembourg	Nc	Nc	161.3	90
Norway	Nc	Nc	13.6	74
Switzerland	Nc	Nc	172.6	62
Canada	Nc	Nc	3.1	77
USA	Nc	Nc	28.7	77

Source: Adapted from *Status Report on European Telework*, 1998. European Commission/National Statistics Offices/Eurostat/Euromonitor.
*Figures are based on a broad definition of teleworking
Nc – no comparable figures

one of the countries recognized as being ahead of Europe on the adoption of teleworking is the USA. It was estimated in 1997 that the USA had 11.1 million employees working at least part-time at home, a rise of nearly 1.5 million on the previous year (European Commission, 1998). These figures are based on a rather restricted definition of teleworking, excluding those working informally from home. Despite this, the figures suggest that around 8.5 per cent of employed people telework (based on 1997 estimates of employed people, Euromonitor, 1999).

One of the most valuable datasets on organizational-level HRM practice is that of the Cranet research network[1]. Examination of the teleworking data from this survey, summarized in Table 2.2, shows the level of use of teleworking as an employment option in organizations (with 200 or more employees) across 12 European countries, Australia and New Zealand. The European data shows Sweden to be by far the greatest adopter, with 47 per cent of medium and large organizations indicating they use telework to some degree. The Netherlands, Finland, Switzerland, the UK and Belgium also show relative high use of this form of work. Looking outside Europe, both Australia (19 per cent of organizations) and New Zealand (20 per cent of organizations) are clearly at the fore in their use of telework. The adoption of other forms of flexibility may also have a positive impact on the promotion of telework. In countries such as the Netherlands, Sweden, Denmark and the UK, where teleworking levels are relatively high, part-time employment is used extensively, and is coupled with a clear trend in the rise of a range of flexible working arrangements (Brewster et al., 1997; Tregaskis, 1999).

One limitation of the statistics is that they tell us little about the number of jobs that are and can be done through teleworking. For example, members of international research and development teams may be located

TABLE 2.2   Percentage of organizations indicating they use teleworking as an employment option, 1995

Country	% of organizations using telework
Sweden	47
Netherlands	24
Finland	14
Switzerland	11
UK	11
Belgium	11
Denmark	9
Germany (former BRD)	9
France	8
Ireland	5
Spain	3
Germany (former DDR)	2
+ Australia	19
*New Zealand	20

Source: Cranet, 1995, + 1996, *1997

thousands of miles from each other, yet work as a team to deliver a specific product or service. As technologies have advanced, they have been paralleled with changes in organizational structures and the expansion of virtual teams (see Lamond, Chapter 3). The pace of change in this field is so rapid that much of the data on teleworking levels is now out of date. Despite these limitations, the statistics are able to indicate national variations in telework practice, with some countries clearly further advanced in take-up than others. In the remaining sections of this chapter, we will examine some of the national context factors that have contributed to the diversity and pace of adoption of teleworking throughout Europe and beyond. These national sources of divergence are important aspects for managers to take into account when considering the viability of teleworking in their organization. The issue of national context is pertinent for managers in international companies who may be considering transferring teleworking practices across national borders. Equally, for those managers seeking to transfer 'good' practice and 'know-how' on teleworking based on the experiences of companies in other countries, this chapter will aid in evaluating the viability of transfer and level of adaptation needed.

Teleworking and the national context

This section explores some of the national context factors that are influential in promoting telework. We will look at teleworking with respect to three features of the national environment:

1. the information society context;
2. employers' and individuals' attitudes to teleworking;
3. the role of government, industrial relations and trade unions.

Teleworking and the information society context

One of the factors that has a significant impact on both demand and supply of teleworking is the information society context (EIRR, 1996, no. 268). By this, we mean the extent to which information technology has become integrated into the everyday lives of people in different societies. Key indicators, for example IT 'spend', the use of mobile phones, access to the Internet and availability of personal computers in peoples' homes, are summarized in Table 2.3.

The USA has by far the greatest IT spend as a percentage of GDP, at 4.08 per cent. Another indicator, in terms of the number of personal computers (PCs) in people's homes, shows that ownership in the USA far outweighs that in Europe (European Commission, 1998; Lillington, 1999). For example, it is estimated that in the USA, 37 in every 100 households have a PC. The northern European average is 19 per hundred, while the highest penetration in any single European country is the UK with 23 per hundred. It is argued that the cost of communications technology has been one of the prime factors that has

TABLE 2.3   The information society context

Country	IT spend as % of GDP in 1996	Mobile phone subscribers as % of total telephone subscribers in 1996	Internet usage as % of population in 1997
Denmark	2.9	26.5	13.1
Netherlands	Nc	Nc	9.0
UK	3.2	11.6	9.5
Finland	Nc	29.1	14.6
Ireland	Nc	Nc	4.1
Sweden	3.4	28.1	15.2
Belgium	Nc	Nc	4.7
Germany	2.1	6.7	6.5
Austria	Nc	Nc	4.6
Portugal	1.4	Nc	1.9
France	2.4	Nc	2.6
Italy	1.4	Nc	2.4
Spain	1.3	Nc	2.2
Greece	0.9	Nc	1.1
USA	4.1	Nc	Nc
EU average	2.2	–	5.4

Source: European Commission, *Status Report on European Trends in Telework* (1998)
Nc – no comparable data available

enabled use and familiarity with information technologies in the USA to spread at such a rapid rate (Lillington, 1999).

Within Europe, Sweden, Denmark, the Netherlands, Finland and the UK consistently appear in the top ranking for figures relating to Internet usage, PC usage, mobile phone penetration and investment in IT. However, the pace of change means that the positioning of these countries is subject to constant change. There is a clear north/south divide in many of these indicators. For example, IT spend tends to be highest in Sweden (3.4 per cent of GDP), the UK (3.2 per cent of GDP) and Denmark (2.9 per cent of GDP), but this is greatly reduced in the southern countries (see Table 2.3). Internet usage is highest for Sweden, followed by Finland, Denmark, the UK and Ireland (see Table 2.3). Figures for PC use show a quite different picture, with Ireland having the highest percentage of white-collar workers using PCs, even though PC use for the whole Ireland population is not even ranked in the top five: Denmark, Sweden, the Netherlands, Finland and the UK (European Commission, 1998). Sweden, Denmark, Finland and the Netherlands tend on the whole to be the greatest users of information technologies.

The availability of equivalent data for the Central and Eastern European countries is particularly poor. However, what is available suggests that Internet usage is, perhaps not surprisingly, low. The European Commission *Status Report on Teleworking* (1998) suggests that the economic conditions would not necessitate a strong demand for teleworking (using a narrower definition of the term). However, the high levels of unemployment, appropriate language skills and good educational standards are conducive to supporting some teleworking applications (e.g. centralized telecentres).

Other issues that play an important part in supporting information technologies at the national level include wealth, affordability, and industrial and occupational structures. Standard of living and purchasing power have an important part to play in the feasibility of teleworking from an individual's point of view. In Northern Europe and the USA, where the information society infrastructure is strong and teleworking levels relatively high, the wealth of the countries is also high compared to Southern Europe and Central and Eastern Europe (see EIU Country Profile Reports). Consequently, the relative cost of a computer for someone in Italy is much higher than for someone in the USA or Sweden. Equally, as pointed out earlier, the actual costs of PCs in the USA are much lower than for Europe (Lillington, 1999). Denmark has seen a rapid rise in the acceptance of telework, which has in part been due to the innovative steps taken by the government towards stimulating the market. This has included the removal of tax on home PCs (European Commission, 1998). Telephone charges also have an impact. In Ireland, the cost of national and international calls has been kept high owing to tight regulation and lack of competition in the industry (European Commission, 1998). However, this is expected to change as a consequence of recent liberalization of the industry. Equally, telecommunications pricing in Austria is high which in part explains the low take-up of teleworking in a relatively wealthy and developed economy (European Commission, 1998). By contrast, in Greece the primary barrier to teleworking is the lack of adequate telecommunications networks. This makes the adoption of telework inefficient for cost reasons (EIRR, 1996, no. 269).

The distribution of organizations across industries within a country can have a profound effect on the relevance and application of telework in that country. Insurance, banking, service companies and telecommunications tend to be the industries most consistently associated with the adoption of teleworking (EIRO, 1998). For example, in Spain and Greece tourism and agriculture make a significant contribution to GDP, whereas in countries such as Sweden these industries are less significant to overall GDP (EIU, 1998a,b,c,). The concept of working from home is less relevant in tourism and agriculture than other industries. In Ireland, while agriculture is still a significant part of the economy, there has been a growth in services and manufacturing (Heraty and Morley, 1998). In particular, call centres owned by multinationals have had a significant impact on teleworking numbers (European Commission, 1998).

At the occupational level, teleworking is often linked to highly qualified white-collar workers with high autonomy, and where knowledge is a significant value-added aspect of the job. This would include programmers, analysts, engineers, architects, travel agents, estate agents, journalists, lawyers and consultants (EIRO, 1998). Looking at national occupational profiles, we can see, for example, that Greece has one of the lowest proportions of information workers in Europe. Consequently, any rise in teleworking in Greece is argued to be related to increases in the numbers of self-employed highly skilled professionals and expansion of the finance sector (EIRR, 1996, no. 269). In Ireland, investment in information technology as a whole is low, although as noted earlier, the use of computers by white-collar workers is among the highest in Europe (European Commission, 1998). This might suggest that tele-working is likely to expand among white-collar workers. There is evidence from the UK and Spain that the occupations affected by teleworking are widening to include white-collar jobs where autonomy and skill levels are not so high, for example secretaries, clerks and data processors (EIRO, 1998). We might argue that this is a reflection of managerial innovation aimed at promoting workforce flexibility.

Finally, issues of physical and social geography cannot be ignored when considering where and why teleworking has spread. It is probably not surprising that in countries such as Finland, Sweden and the USA, where the population density is low, teleworking is fairly high (see again Table 2.1). As with other indicators of the information society context, however, geographical characteristics cannot be considered in isolation. For example, Ireland, Greece and Spain also have low population density statistics, but lag behind countries such as the UK, the Netherlands and Denmark where the population density is much higher. In Japan and some parts of the USA, the risk of earthquakes has encouraged organizations to decentralize, promoting remote office working (Sato and Spinks, 1998). Clearly, under such conditions the motivation to adopt teleworking is driven less by demands for organizational flexibility and more by necessity for organizational effectiveness.

Employers' and individuals' attitudes to teleworking

Employer attitudes towards using telework as a form of corporate employment and individual attitudes towards operating as a teleworker are two of the biggest factors affecting the take-up of telework. For example, take-up in Austria is low relative to the availability of opportunity (EIRR, 1996, no. 268). In other words, the 'supply side' by far outstrips the demand. In addition to the relative high cost of telecommunications, one of the primary explanations for this trend is reported to be the attitude of indi-viduals towards teleworking (European Commission, 1998). However, there is evidence that individual attitudes are becoming more positive, particularly among young people, with 77 per cent of those under 30 years of age viewing teleworking positively (European Commission, 1998 p. 37). In 1990, Empirica reported the results from a survey of 16,000 households in West Germany, France, Italy and the UK on attitudes towards teleworking (Huws et al., 1990). The results showed considerable variation across the countries. The West German sample showed the least interest in adopting telework, followed by Italy and France, while the UK showed the most interest. Although this survey was carried out nearly 10 years ago, we can see an asso-ciation between those negative attitudes of the early 1990s and low relative take-up of teleworking in those countries today (see Table 2.1).

Undoubtedly individual attitudes are intertwined with other contextual factors. For example, in France, work and individual contributions are firmly rooted within notions of working time and the culture of office-based work is strong. Many commentators have frequently referred to the significance of hierarchy in the control and organization of work (Barsoux and Lawrence, 1994). Thus, some fundamental shifts in how telework is construed will be needed if teleworking is to gain widespread acceptance in France. Teleworking is also dogged to some extent by old views of homeworking (i.e. piece-rate working), creating some reservations. For example, in the Netherlands teleworking tends to be associated with this older form of work, and legislation and regulation for teleworkers is based around this traditional form of homeworking, which is often inappropriate (European Commission, 1998).

The higher incidence of teleworking in Sweden compared to other countries may be a reflection of the collectivist orientation prevalent in Swedish working and social arrangements (Wåglund and Lindström, 1997). In Germany, the vocational education system promotes competencies and values related to the social dimension of work and so, to the extent that teleworking does not fit comfortably within this context, adoption has been slow (Durrenburger *et al.*, 1995). Gillespie *et al.* (1995) argue that in the case of the UK the migration of knowledge workers away from cities to rural areas, for quality of life reasons, has been a factor in the spread of teleworking. Such conditions within a country can have a profound effect on positive or negative attitudes towards teleworking.

Teleworking has also been expected by many to be a female-dominated employment option, as is the case with other forms of flexible work, such as part-time work. However, evidence from the Dutch labour market, which has the highest female workforce participation rates in Europe, suggests that unlike other flexible work options (e.g. part-time work, term-time working), telework is not viewed as a particularly favourable option by women as many want to work away from the home (cf. Standen, Chapter 9). Huws (1993), in a study of teleworking in Britain, also found the myth of teleworking being more popular among females to be unfounded. This suggests that the benefits of the flexibility offered through telework are not gender specific, but are linked more to the job role and the reorganization of work.

Attitudes towards teleworking have been closely linked to public policy on road transport and pollution. Consequently, in some countries, such as the Netherlands, governments are keen to promote teleworking for environmental reasons (EIRR, 1996, no. 271). Evidence from the USA suggests that environmental concerns associated with car use and road congestion are no longer major drivers towards the use of teleworking from the organization's perspective (de Pous, 1998). This is partly due to the very prominent and central role of the car industry within the US business markets. The primary concern of organizations is the financial consequences of teleworking. Financial inducements to encourage more employers and individuals to adopt teleworking as a form of employment may be a more effective motivator. If wider societal benefits are ever to be realized, greater efforts need to be made to stimulate both the demand and supply sides of teleworking.

The role of government, industrial relations and trade unions

One area of concern for governments, pressure groups and individuals has been the implications of teleworking in the light of current employment legislation. Little employment regulation exists specifically for teleworkers, and teleworking is not a legal category like 'self-employed'. In most countries throughout the world, teleworkers are considered either as employees where an employment relationship exists, or as non-employees where a business relationship exists. Depending on the employment status, either labour law is applied to teleworkers, as in the case of an employment relationship, or company law is applied, as in the case of a business relationship (EIRO, 1998). Therefore, the employment status of such workers can influence the adoption of teleworking. In many countries, a large proportion of those doing 'telecommutable' jobs are not employed by an organization but instead are self-employed and work as a contractor for organizations. However, the legal and tax status of teleworkers with an employment relationship or business relationship varies considerably from country to country.

Issues can become even more complicated when the teleworking contract is defined as a business relationship, but an employment relationship exists, although it may be difficult to demonstrate. In such cases, some countries recommend that employers adopt self-employed legal status to define those people who are 'formally and personally independent' from them but 'economically dependent' in their work (EIRO, 1998, p. i). Consequently, the legal status of 'self-employed' is used in many countries to define teleworking. This too has its problems. In Ireland, the confusion over the distinction between 'employed' and 'self-employed' has made employers reluctant to give work to self-employed teleworkers. Equally, if individuals work from home then these premises may be considered as business premises and subject to additional taxes. Further, self-employed individuals usually have less widespread employment protection or rights in terms of pensions and social security benefits. In Germany, the lack of alternative and equal levels of employment regulation for the self-employed compared to the employed or unemployed has sparked considerable debate and concern. At the same time, protection is given to independent teleworkers via the Homeworking Act (Heimarbeitsgesetz), which applies to all work carried out at home, and to dependent (e.g. employed) teleworkers who are covered by working time, regulation and collective employment rights (EIRR, 1996, no. 269). In highly regulated environments such as Germany, it will be important that potential teleworkers see their employment rights and social security benefits or pensions protected in line with other forms of employment. The ILO proposed convention on homework promotes equal treatment of these workers; however, it does not include self-employed homeworkers. In 1990, Greece introduced a new employment act to ensure that self-employed individuals would be covered by collective agreements (European Foundation for the Improvement of Living and Working Conditions, 1997) and this may stimulate the growth of teleworking among this group of workers.

The inequity in employment terms and conditions of home-based workers compared to their office-based counterparts is one of the prime reasons that trade unions have traditionally been opposed to teleworking or, at the very least, viewed it with some reservations. However, in some countries this is changing. Attitudes are becoming more positive and action is being taken to put forward guidance and organize protection in recognition that many union members actually wish to telework (European Commission, 1998; EIRO, 1998). Consequently, the role of collective bargaining in the regulation of teleworking varies considerably across Europe.

Collective agreements do not tend to regulate teleworking in Belgium, Finland, Greece, Luxembourg, the Netherlands or Portugal (EIRO, 1998). In France, Germany, Ireland, the UK, Austria and Norway, sectoral agreements on telework are marginal (e.g. Austria had its first sectoral agreement signed in 1997 in the mineral oil industry), but there has been a rise in company-level agreements (EIRR, 1996, no. 268). Only in Sweden, Italy and Denmark does bargaining play a much stronger role in the regulation of telework at both the company and sectoral level (EIRO, 1998). It would seem that in countries where trade union attitude has become more favourable towards teleworking, efforts are being made to provide safeguards for employees and to stimulate uptake.

In countries where the industrial relations tradition is less regulated and organizational autonomy is greater, stimulation of teleworking supply and demand operates very differently. In the USA, for example, in order to take advantage of collective representation, a number of new commercial organizations for the self-employed are emerging where, for an annual fee, they receive access to health and insurance cover in addition to telecommunication technologies (de Pous, 1998). The information technology industry has a number of these new types of organization which in addition to providing the self-employed teleworkers with business support (e.g. advice on tax returns, insurance etc.) also puts the contractor in touch with potential clients, thus operating like a traditional temporary employment agency.

There is thus a difference in approach in how best to provide support for teleworkers: a) through legislation or b) through sectoral and company agreements. Many feel teleworking is still an evolving employment arrangement and, as such, it is too early to try to apply legislation. Using sectoral or company agreements would provide greater flexibility to apply protection to the moving target that is telework.

Conclusions

Teleworking is a new and still evolving approach to working. This chapter has demonstrated some of the macro socio-technical, economic and culturally based issues that have been affecting take-up and salience of teleworking. For managers considering implementing a teleworking system these issues need to be borne in mind. In terms of the information society context, the cost and current penetration of information and communications technologies (ICTs) can affect the feasibility of introducing telework methods. Equally, where individuals are spread out within a country or across countries or where traffic congestion is a problem, teleworking may give the manager an advantage in the effective utilization of organizational intellectual capital.

While there is value in learning lessons from other countries, management solutions frequently fail due to lack of sensitivity to context-specific issues. Therefore, it is important to consider baseline attitudes toward teleworking and where possible remove any barriers. Teleworking may be rapidly accepted in an environment where attitudes are favourable but resistance may meet the manager elsewhere. Within Europe, the members of the European Union have recognized the divergence in employment law and social security conditions hindering the acceptance of teleworking, although there is a reluctance among many policy makers to move toward further regulation in this area. This means that employees need to take responsibility, individually or collectively, for negotiating contracts that compensate them according to any change in their employment status. Employers then need to consider tailor-made teleworking solutions that meet the needs of their company and are attractive enough to encourage employees to work in this way. It remains to be seen under what conditions it will be possible to develop transnational versus culturally sensitive teleworking management systems.

Notes

[1]Cranet is a group of 22 European, US, Canadian, Japanese, Australian and New Zealand Universities who carry out an international comparative survey of HRM practice. The survey was first undertaken in 1990 with five European countries. Since then five successive rounds of data collection have been conducted, with expansion of the network beyond Europe. For a review of the evolution of the project see Brewster and Hegewisch (1994) and Brewster *et al.* (1996).

References

Barsoux, J.-L. and Lawrence, P. (1994) *Management in France*. London: Cassell.

Brewster, C. and Hegewisch, A. (1994) *Policy and Practice in European Human Resource Management: The Price Waterhouse Survey*. Routledge, London.

Brewster, C., Tregaskis, O., Hegewisch, A. and Mayne, L. (1996) Comparative Research in Human Resource Management. *International Journal of Human Resource Management*, 7, 585–604.

Brewster, C., Mayne, L., Tregaskis, O., Parsons, D., Atterbury, S., Hegewisch, A., Soler, C., Aparicio Valverde, M., Picq, T., Weber, W., Kabst, R., Wåglund, M. and Lindström, K. (1997) *Working Time and Contract Flexibility*. Report prepared for Directorate General V of the Commission of the European Union. Centre for European HRM.

De Pous, V.A. (1998) *Teleworking: Management Summary Report*. Prepared for Directorate General XIII of the Commission of the European Union. Distributed at the Third International Workship and Conference on Teleworking in Turku, Finland, September, 1998.

Durrenburger, G., Bieri, L., Jaeger, C. and Dahinden, U. (1995) Telework and Vocational Contact. *Technology Studies*, **2**, 104–31.

Euromonitor (1999) *International Marketing Data and Statistics 1999* (23rd edn). Euromonitor: London.

European Industrial Relations Observatory (EIRO) (1998). *Teleworking and Industrial Relations in Europe*, November, i–iv.

European Industrial Relations Review (EIRR) (1996) *Teleworking in Europe: Part One*, **268**, 17–20.

European Industrial Relations Review (EIRR) (1996) *Teleworking in Europe: Part Two*, **269**, 18–21.

European Industrial Relations Review (EIRR) (1996) *Teleworking in Europe: Part Three*, **271**, 18–23.

European Commission (1998) *Status Report on European Telework*. Luxembourg: Office for Official Publications of the European Communities.

European Foundation for the Improvement of Living and Working Conditions (1997) *The Social Implications of Teleworking*. Luxembourg: Office for Official Publications for the European Communities.

Economic Intelligence Unit (EIU) (1998a) *Country Profile Sweden 1998–99*. London: EIU.

Economic Intelligence Unit (EIU) (1998b) *Country Profile Spain 1998–99*. London: EIU.

Economic Intelligence Unit (EIU) (1998c) *Country Profile Greece 1998–99*. London: EIU.

Gillespie, A.E., Richardson, R. and Cornford, J. (1995) *Review of Teleworking in Britain: Implications for Public Policy*. London: Report to the Parliamentary Office of Science and Technology.

Heraty, N. and Morley, M. (1998) The national learning environment: Ireland. Research report sponsored under the European Commission's Fourth Framework Research Programme. University of Limerick, Department of Personnel and Employment Relations, Ireland.

Huws, U., Korte, W.B. and Robinson, S. (1990) *Telework: towards the Elusive Office*. Wiley: Chichester.

Huws, U. (1993) *Teleworking in Britain*. Research Series no. 18. Sheffield: Employment Department.

Lillington, K. (1999) PC prices hamper information age. *Irish Financial Times*, 9 April, 59.

Sato, K. and Spinks, W.A. (1998) Telework and Crisis Management in Japan. In P.J. Jackson and J.M. Van der Wielen (eds) *Teleworking: International Perspectives, from Telecommuting to the Virtual organization*. London: Routledge.

Tregaskis, O. (1999) The boundaries of converging management practice: Cross national comparisons of contingent employment. Symposium paper presented at the American Academy of Management Meeting, Chicago, 9–11 August .

Wåglund, M. and Lindström, K. (1997) Swedish Report. In C. Brewster, L. Mayne, O.Tregaskis, Parsons, S. Atterbury, A. Hegewisch, C. Soler, M. Aparicio Valverde, T. Picq, W. Weber, R. Kabst, M. Wåglund and K. Lindström, *Working Time and Contract Flexibility*. Report prepared for Directorate General V of the Commission of the European Union. Cranfield, Beds: Centre for European HRM, Cranfield University.

Chapter 3

Organizational structures that support telework

David Lamond

Discussions about teleworking to date have focused on telework itself and the forms it may take, more than the organizational context or structure within which it occurs. In part, this reflects the focus of practitioners and researchers to date. That is not to say that people aren't interested in organizational structure – a search of the ABI/Inform research database, using the terms 'organization' and 'structure', identified 521 references in 1998 alone. On the other hand, a search of the database from 1994–1998, using the keywords 'teleworking', 'organization' and 'structure' together, identified no references. It would appear that people talk about organization structures and teleworking, but not in the same sentence – telework is something you do *in* organizations; you do not structure organizations around teleworking.

The purpose of this chapter is to examine specifically the relationship between organizational structure and teleworking, and so identify the organizational structures that are most likely to support teleworking. We begin by considering organizations and organizational structure in general. We will then concentrate on two issues related to organizational structure – teams and coordination – reflecting the current preoccupation with teams as an organizational form on the one hand, and the reality of trying to harmonize the activities of disparate groups, separated in geography and time, on the other.

Organizations and organizational structure

In the simplest terms, organization is the bringing together of a group of individuals to accomplish a given task (Ensign, 1998). Organisational *structure* refers to the way in which that group is divided into smaller groups, responsible for distinct tasks, and then how coordination is achieved between them (Mintzberg, 1979). When we talk about organizational structure, we are not just alluding to organizational charts, with their boxes and lines. Rather, we are referring to the policies, prescriptions of authority and hierarchies of responsibility; the allocations of work roles and administrative mechanisms that allow organizations to conduct, coordinate and control their work activities (Rapert and Wren, 1998).

Organization design has developed as a discipline area since we slowly began to think of new and different ways of thinking about how we best organize to meet our customers' needs in a changing environment (see, for example, Burns and Stalker, 1961). The empirical research of Lawrence and Lorsch (1967) provides us with an important insight for our discussion here. They found that the most appropriate organizational structure is not only contingent on the environmental demands or conditions that confront the organization, but also the types of work being performed. This reminds us that how we divide the work tasks will be a function, at least in part, of how we are going to carry out those tasks. In this regard, Peter Drucker (1998) recently cautioned us once more against looking for the 'one best way' of organizing.

Over the past decade, we have been witness to a number of trends which have affected organizational structure – downsizing; delayering; process re-engineering; replacement of traditional functional departments with team-based or project-based structures; the shift to a core/periphery model with a greater role for contingent workers; growth in inter-organizational networks; and boundaryless designs (Ashkenas et al., 1995; Dess et al., 1995; McKinley et al., 1998). These all point to a rise in teleworking. The reasons appear to be twofold.

On the one hand, the rise in knowledge work and the increased sophistication of information technology make it easier for organizations to develop structures that transcend traditional space and time limits (Reich, 1992; Handy, 1995). These structures can often be characterized as loose federations of groups and individuals. Building on the contingency approach to organizational structure (Lawrence and Lorsch, 1967; Dess et al., 1995), it could be expected that such flexible, 'organic' organizations are more likely to move towards teleworking and are more likely to have effective teleworkers. The reciprocal relationship is likely to exist here too, as growth in teleworking encourages wider experimentation with flexible structures. For example, Travic (1998) found a positive relationship between the amount of IT usage and the existence of non-traditional organizational structures, and invoked the notion of an 'organic, informated organization'.

On the other hand, teleworking might be introduced by organizations where the primary attraction is the promised cost reductions through downsizing and delayering the organization, and geographical relocation of the remaining employees and functions. Here there may be a distinct lack of interest in flexibility issues and notions of 're-engineering' may be code for cost-cutting. The impact on teleworking is likely to be quite different to that of the organic orientation and so we need to explore carefully the reasons for introducing teleworking.

The consequences of these factors are different for the different forms of telework we identified in Chapter 1. For example, the growth of 'virtual teams' may shift teleworking more towards a full-time option for high knowledge intensity workers, while the greater use of a contingent workforce is likely to see a rise in low knowledge intensity teleworkers. We might also expect a rise in both home and nomadic working (as opposed to telecottage and remote office working) in virtual organizations as workers are tied less to one organization or location of the main office.

Before we deal with teams and their coordination, an important point of clarification here is that regarding the blurring of 'teleworking' as a form of work and 'virtual organizations' as forms of organizing (cf. Adler and Zirger, 1998; Dickerson, 1998; Venkatraman and Henderson, 1998). We note that 'virtual organizations' are variously defined as:

- a move from a unitary business form to a 'hub' or centre of a business linked to a collection of independent functional entities by a series of contracts (Dickerson, 1998);
- a cross-functional, cross-divisional team that is organized for a specific project (Adler and Zirger, 1998);
- 'not a distinct structure (like functional, divisional, or matrix). Instead, we treat virtualness as a strategic characteristic applicable to every organization' (Venkatraman and Henderson, 1998, p. 33).

The first of these is the more commonly accepted definition, with the distinction between the two forms of organization – unitary and hub – summarized in Figure 3.1. A typical product manufacturing and sales company (a), for example, could outsource all its functions except, say, the marketing function (b) and operate as if it was 'virtually' the same company as in (a).

Of course, none of these organizational forms or approaches necessarily requires the implementation of teleworking to be described as a virtual organization. Equally, a firm could be engaged entirely in teleworking, as a form of work, and still not be a virtual organization. For example, a pharmaceutical company with geographically dispersed teams of salespeople, connected to the head office and to each other by mobile phone, fax and e-mail, has a significant number of its staff engaging in telework, but it remains a unitary organization nonetheless. Malone and Laubacher (1998) give us a good example of how teleworking and virtual organization might combine in their discussion of the transformation of large, permanent corporations into flexible, temporary networks of electronically connected freelancers – Malone and Laubacher (1998) refer to them as *e-lancers*. These individuals constitute fluid and temporary networks to produce and sell goods and services, and when they finish the job, the network dissolves.

We need to draw the distinction too between organizations in which teleworking may occur and organizations that have been created/shaped with telework in mind. Just as the way organizations are designed will determine whether they encourage or crush creativity (Amabile, 1998), so their design and operation will encourage or crush teleworking. We might predict that those organizations that we have referred to as having an organic orientation would encourage, while the mechanistic cost-cutters will crush (cf. Standen, Chapter 4).

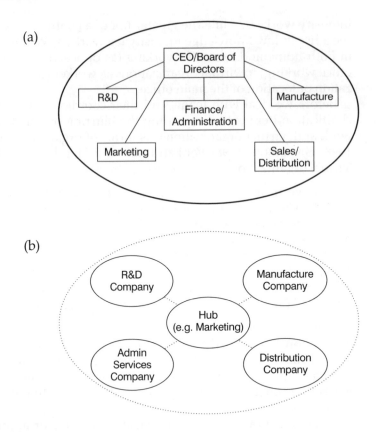

FIGURE 3.1   Unitary (a) and virtual (b) organizational forms of a product manufacturing and sales company

Teams and teleworking

Teams and team-based work systems have been the dominant organizational initiative of the past decade for enhancing the organization's ability to achieve its goals (Townsend *et al.*, 1998). When teams work effectively, they can be paragons of productivity, efficiency and employee satisfaction; but when they are dysfunctional, neither employer nor employee is content. West (1997) has suggested that often this is due to the difference between having teams in organizations and having organizations constructed round the existence of teams. In the latter, teams *feel* empowered and have skill development, as well as self-management, to be productive and satisfied. The question for us then is 'When are teams appropriate, for what forms of telework?'

Townsend *et al.* (1998) provide us with many of the answers to this question in their discussion about 'virtual teams', which are linked primarily through advanced information and communications technologies (ICTs). These teams have developed as a response to the challenges associated with downsized and lean (flat) organizations and the geographical and organizational dispersal of employees which has resulted from fewer layers of centralized, hierarchical management structures (Townsend *et al.*, 1998).[1] Their existence has been enabled by the developments in ICTs, which, as we noted earlier, have also encouraged organizations to experiment with new organizational forms.

Virtual teams are 'groups of geographically and/or organizationally dispersed coworkers that are assembled using a combination of telecommunications and information technologies to accomplish an organizational task' (Townsend *et al.*, 1998, p. 17). These teams can be temporary or permanent, with fluid, evolving membership. The challenges which confront those adopting both a team approach and teleworking as the form of work are also present in traditional work settings, and all affect the environment in which individual members must operate (Townsend *et al.*, 1998). Virtual team members still need traditional teamwork – effective communication skills, goal clarity and performance orientation. As for any team, managers need to establish clear expectations about performance and criteria for assessing success, and there is a need for schedules for reports, interim deliverables and the final product. The changes in the type of work and the context within which the work is carried out, however, will affect the way team members conduct work, communicate with each other and express themselves (Townsend *et al.*, 1998). Members of virtual teams need to:

- learn new ways to express themselves and understand others in an environment with a 'diminished sense of presence';
- develop superior team participation skills, *inter alia*, because fluid membership requires quick assimilators;
- gain proficiency in a variety ICTs;
- develop communication and cultural sensitivity skills (geographical dispersion may cross national (and cultural) boundaries).

In their discussion of virtual teams, Townsend *et al.* (1998) focus only on location and the use of ICTs. In doing so, they observe that telework is usually limited to relatively independent job categories that involve low levels of collaboration. They argue that the 'virtual team' format can expand telework's potential by allowing employees involved in highly collaborative teamwork to participate from remote locations. If we understand their meaning correctly, they are referring in the first instance to a subset of teleworkers engaged in low knowledge intensity work (see Chapter 1). The second group to which they refer, those involved in highly collaborative teamwork, appears to be a subset of those we describe as engaged in high knowledge intensity work (Chapter 1). Given our approach to teleworking, we would incorporate the notion of 'virtual teams' as an approach to structuring and managing high knowledge intensity teleworkers with high degrees of intra-organizational communication. It is unlikely that 'virtual teams', at least in the way Townsend *et al.* (1998) have characterized them, would be a useful structure for those whose telework activities involve relatively low knowledge intensity jobs with low levels of intra-organizational communication.

Coordination

As we noted earlier, Lawrence and Lorsch (1967) highlighted the value of adopting a contingency approach to organizing. They also found that structurally differentiated units (now teams) are likely to differ concerning their goals, time perspectives and interpersonal methods of interaction, and the degree to which their structure is formalized. Further, they found that patterns of communication and information flows in organizations often reinforce the isolation of the units from each other, such that most units pay little attention to the organization. In a similar vein to Mintzberg (1979), we might observe that teaming produces coordination within the team, at the expense of coordination between teams.

Ensign (1998) argues that, in order to design an organization that can provide for coordination between units (teams), there is a need for:

- changes in the way units are grouped and coordinated, including the use of lateral mechanisms and processes;
- collaboration and cooperation among units – those who are directly involved in inter-unit exchanges and sharing to be involved in planning and decision making;
- management skills and abilities devoted to managing interdependence;
- appropriate ways of handling the conflicts that inevitably arise between groups;
- integrative systems that encourage exchange and sharing.

Here, we see another example of how we can describe teleworking as both cause and effect. Scattering of team members may mean that effective supervision and control appears problematic. However, the rich communication environment provided by ICTs enables greater managerial monitoring rather than less, relative to the traditional environment. For example, the manager can review archived recordings of team meetings to assess member contribution and team progress (Townsend *et al.*, 1998). Indeed, this environment also provides a strong medium for self-managed teams – because information can be shared instantly and inexpensively among many people in many locations, individuals can manage themselves and coordinate their efforts through their electronic links (Malone and Laubacher, 1998; see also Soloman and Templer, 1994). If communication is the social glue that ties members, teams and organizations together (Rapert and Wren, 1998), then teleworkers can overcome the geographic and time dispersion they may experience, to the extent that their information and communication technologies provide them with access to an enriched communication medium (see Harper, Chapter 6).

Organizational policy on teleworking: an afterword

The future of teleworking as a form of work and virtual organizations as *the* form of organizations is not clear. Some are using terms such as 'flat', 'employee-empowered', 'shared services' and 'flexible' to describe the 21st century organization (Greco, 1998). Meanwhile, Jermier (1998) has suggested that many of the recent technological changes, managerial innovations and organizational experiments, which have been hailed as revolutionary or paradigm-breaking in both the academic and popular press, are merely fads. Time will tell.

In the meantime, we conclude this discussion on organizational structure with a brief consideration about an important teleworking policy. We noted earlier that organizational structure includes organizational policies regarding the conduct, coordination and control of work activities. One of the policies that organizations need to consider is whether teleworking will be a voluntary or mandatory work form.

Typically, mandatory telework programmes are driven by business process improvement and are targeted at sales and professional service staff, involving a re-engineering of their work processes, while voluntary programmes are a response to employee need for flexibility. Where organizations offer telework on a voluntary basis, as a form of flexible work arrangement, telework is usually employee-driven, with the goal of improved work/family balance and the organization being the 'employer of choice' (Froggatt, 1998). Does that mean that mandatory is 'bad' and voluntary is 'good'? It depends.

As is the case in the implementation of many human resource strategies, if a programme mandates employee participation, it usually mandates management support and provides the appropriate structure, training, equipment, network, maintenance, funding, and so on. On the other hand, voluntary programmes often suffer from 'voluntary inconsistent commitment' from management, resulting in resistance, lack of funding, inconsistent implementation, etc. Many voluntary teleworking programmes have been just one component of a flexible work policy that, although available to staff, is rarely promoted or supported in a significant way (Froggatt, 1998).

Two US companies, NCR and Nortel, have implemented successful 'virtual office' (teleworking) strategies, but have done so in quite different ways. NCR introduced its programme on a mandatory basis, while teleworking at Nortel is voluntary. Froggatt (1998) describes the NCR telework programme as part of a comprehensive, integrated approach to sales and productivity, well supported in terms of management commitment and funding. Resistance was dispelled through training and education programmes, and an appeals process. Participants are able to choose among at least three workplace options – a client site, home, and a shared workstation in a field office. Nortel's programme is no less business focused, but once management made the decision to implement the programme, it set about promoting telework as a viable option. Nortel's programme is supported by a 10-member, cross-functional team dedicated to the promotion and administration of the teleworking effort (with another 10–15 others working on technical support on a part-time basis). There are regularly scheduled educational programmes and full-scale 'home office' examples that employees can test. Senior management demonstrates its commitment, *inter alia*, by several vice presidents being active teleworkers (Froggatt, 1998). It appears that whether the programme is mandatory or not is less important than ensuring that the organization provides the requisite ICT and financial resources, and employees receive appropriate training and development. These, in turn, need to be underpinned by a demonstrable level of senior management support for teleworking.

We have considered in this chapter organizational structure and telework, with our focus on teams and their coordination. It is clear that telework is both cause and effect in relation to these matters – the development of teleworking and its associated ICTs have been encouraged by, but also enabled, new organizational structures. However, we should not lose sight of the fact that teleworking is neither identical with virtuality, nor restricted to virtual organizations. Teleworking is not exclusive to certain kinds of 'new' work and certain kinds of 'new' organizational structures. Telework is already an established form of work in existing organizations. It supports and is supported by different organizational forms. Regardless of the organizational structure, we should be mindful of what Drucker (1998) describes as a universal principle of organization – people must know and understand the organizational structure in which they are to work.

Notes

[1]Although there are, no doubt, many sales managers, for example, who would be surprised to find that the mobile sales teams they have been managing for many years can now be considered as 'virtual teams'. As far as possible, we will ignore the 'hype' about *virtual* this, that and the other.

References

Adler, T.R. and Zirger, B.J. (1998) Organizational learning: Implications of a virtual research and development organization. *American Business Review*, **16**, 51–60.

Amabile, T.M. (1998) How to kill creativity. *Harvard Business Review*; **76**, 76–87.

Ashkenas, R., Ulrich, D., Jick, T. and Kerr, S. (1995) *The Boundaryless Organization: Breaking the Chains of Organizational Structure*. San Francisco: Jossey-Bass.

Burns, T. and Stalker, G.M. (1961) *The Management of Innovation*. New York: Tavistock.

Dess, G.G., Rasheed, A.M.A., McLaughlin, K.J. and Priem, R.L. (1995) The new corporate architecture. *Academy of Management Executive*, **9**, August, 7–20.

Dickerson, C.M. (1998) Virtual organizations: from dominance to opportunism. *New Zealand Journal of Industrial Relations*, **23**, 35–46.

Drucker, P.F. (1998) Management's new paradigms. *Forbes*, **162**, October 5, 152–77.

Ensign, P.C. (1998) Interdependence, coordination, and structure in complex organizations: implications for organization design. *The Mid-Atlantic Journal of Business*, **34**, 5–22.

Froggatt, C.C. (1998) Telework: whose choice is it anyway? *Facilities Design & Management*, Spring, 18–21

Greco, J. (1998) Designing for the 21st century. *The Journal of Business Strategy*, **19**, 34–7.

Handy, C. (1995) Trust and the virtual organization. *Harvard Business Review*, **73**, 40–50.

Jermier, J.M. (1998) Introduction: critical perspectives on organizational control. *Administrative Science Quarterly*, **43**, 235–56.

Lawrence, P.R. and Lorsch, J.W. (1967) *Organization and Environment: Managing Differentiation and Integration*. Boston, MA: Graduate School of Business, Harvard University.

Malme, T.W. and Laubacher, R.J. (1988) The dawn of the e-lance economy. Harvard Business Review, **76**, 145–52.

McKinley, W., Mone, M.A. and Barker, V.L. (1998) Some ideological foundations of organizational downsizing, *Journal of Management Inquiry*, **7**, 198–212.

Mintzberg, H. (1979) *The Structuring of Organizations*. Englewood Cliffs, NJ: Prentice-Hall.

Rapert, M.I. and Wren, B.M. (1998) Reconsidering organizational structure: A dual perspective of frameworks and processes, *Journal of Managerial Issues*, **10**, 287–302.

Reich, R. (1992) *The Work of Nations*, New York: Vintage.

Soloman, N.A. and Templer, A.J. (1994) Development of non-traditional work sites: telecommuting, *Inform*, February, 42–4.

Townsend, A.M., DeMarie, S. and Hendrickson, A.R. (1998) Virtual teams: Technology and the workplace of the future, *Academy of Management Executive*, **12**, August, 17–29.

Travic, B. (1998) Information aspects of new organizational designs: Exploring the non-traditional organization, *Journal of the American Society for Information Science*, **49**, 1224–44.

Venkatraman, N. and Henderson, J.C. (1998) Real strategies for virtual organizing, *Sloan Management Review*, **40**, 33–48.

West, M.A. (1997) Reflexivity and revolution in-groups at work. Presented at the 2nd Australian Industrial and Organizational Psychology Conference, Melbourne, 27–29 June.

Chapter 4

Organizational culture and telework

Peter Standen

In recent years the notion of organizational culture has become a popular expla-nation of why some firms are more successful than others (e.g. Peters and Waterman, 1982). In today's highly competitive business environment, how culture aids or constrains organizational innovation is particularly important. Managers contemplating telework would be wise to consider culture, and in this chapter we examine its influence on the decision to use telework, the business goals for telework, and the types of employees that will be involved. Whether telework can, in turn, influence organizational culture is also considered.

Although the concept of culture has proven difficult to define, it generally refers to the set of shared beliefs, values, norms or assumptions that arise when a group of people has a shared history (Schein, 1990). Cultures are passed on to new members, eventually becoming habitual guides to perceiving, thinking and feeling. Culture provides meaning, stability and comfort to individuals. As well as reflecting the organization's past, cultures are influenced by values in the wider community, through regulations imposed by governments, norms embedded in the industry, or explicit copying of other organizations (Powell and DiMaggio, 1991). In these ways, culture explains aspects of organizations not accounted for by structure, strategy, management style or the economic environment.

Culture in the adoption of telework

Strong assumptions about management and work make some organizations less amenable to telework than others, and managers considering telework need to assess the type of culture they inhabit, the types of telework that fit it, and what cultural barriers need to be overcome. Introducing telework in a way that works against organizational norms and attitudes is guaranteed to fail, as illustrated by a pilot programme in the US Army (McDavid, 1985). Although the participants and their managers considered the programme successful, it was ultimately rejected by senior staff because it contravened norms about being *seen* to be working. This is not an isolated event, and reminds us also that organizations may have multiple subcultures with conflicting values.

Cultures that inhibit telework

Early writers expected that the capabilities of new information technology would make telework much more widespread than it is today (e.g. Nilles *et al.*, 1976), and futurists and advocates still tend to undervalue the influence of cultural assumptions about management and work. Table 4.1 shows some assumptions that are widely held by society, regulatory bodies, managers and employees.

A major organizational impediment to telework is managerial concern about losing control of workers when they are out of sight (Kraut, 1987; Olson, 1989; Wilson, 1991). This attitude can be traced to particular factors in the historical evolution of work. The modern office is a fairly recent development, having become the dominant form of work organization only in this century. Its chief management principles are still evolving from the factory model founded on hierarchical control (Weber, 1964) and fragmentation of work into discrete tasks requiring little skill and, hence, having lower labour costs (Taylor, 1911). Recent decades have seen a reaction against this bureaucratic and technical style of management, with the human relations and socio-technical schools turning attention to the social side of the organization and, in particular, to the value of a flexible and committed workforce in turbulent business environments (e.g. Trist, 1981).

An approach to management that gives workers greater discretion over the work process, focuses on outcomes and offers more holistic jobs is clearly better suited to telework than one based on hierarchy and fragmentation. So far, however, the 'worker empowerment' paradigm has not made the impact that its advocates hoped for. Family-friendly work practices such as permanent part-time work, flexitime or job sharing are an example, often said to be 'win-win' strategies that help businesses maintain productivity and

TABLE 4.1   Sources of expectations about telework

Society	Work is performed between 9 and 5 in an office
	Work at home is low status, income-supplementation
	Unions: work at home may be exploitative
Regulatory bodies	Health and safety regulations
	Industrial relations laws
	Local government rules on work at home
Managers	Subordinates must be directly controlled
	Supervisors should be seen to be supervising
	Employees need to participate in organizational culture
	The work process should be visible
	Work is confined to business hours
	Workers should convey a corporate image
	The work process is interruptible
Co-workers	Teleworkers have an additional privilege
	Teleworkers are not serious about their career
	Teleworkers are not available

retain experienced and committed workers by giving them greater discretion over work hours. However, these options are still available only to a small proportion of the workforce in Europe and the USA (Simkin and Hillage 1992; Fierman, 1994), due largely to managers' concerns about losing control over work time and coordination (Blyton, 1986; Fierman, 1994). Telework challenges managerial control more than most of these practices, and it remains one of the least used options (Brewster *et al.*, 1994). The problem goes beyond individual managers' attitudes; management systems, such as those concerned with human resources or financial management, often assume that employees are under continuous direct control and are not equipped to deal with exceptions. Control remains a fundamental value in many corporate cultures today.

Another illustration of the influence of managerial values is the way technology has been used to increase control over teleworkers where freeing them from control might have improved productivity. Computer technology now provides the opportunity for very precise monitoring of activity in some jobs. Telephone call centres, for example, openly display real-time statistics on operator calls, discouraging employees from taking breaks, even brief ones for socializing or rest. These systems create such a strong competitive pressure that most employees last only a few months. In other firms the same technology has been used to allow operators to work from home with discretion over the moment-to-moment work process, and monitoring only on overall productivity: Teleworking operators in one firm studied by the author had higher productivity and remained longer with the organization, saving on the significant costs of recruitment, training, and supervision time.

The central value of control can, therefore, be seen in managers' styles, office systems and the way technology is used. As well, organizations are also social groups where social relations and events influence behaviour, where symbols are used to shape attitudes, and where individuals assert their status over others. Even the physical appearance of an office may be used to increase identification with the organization or work group. These forms of influence are difficult when employees are not confined to a single work site. As Margrethe Olson has written:

> Organizational culture dictates a commitment to the organization as a place. Companies incur tremendous expense providing facilities in which an employee can feel a sense of belonging and safety, with health facilities, libraries, natural surroundings, as well as cafeterias and parking lots. Such trappings are designed to keep employees 'in' (1988, p. 98)

There are also numerous ways that telework challenges assumptions about work. Working in casual clothes, at odd hours, in a home office or lounge does not convey a 'professional' image. If employees think management requires direct supervision, managers whose subordinates cannot be seen may be deemed to be ineffective. Empty desks might suggest inefficient resource use rather than greater productivity or better customer service. Employees who do not participate in office networks might be considered less than serious about their work or careers. Such issues cause managers to be concerned about the messages telework sends to other employees, to clients and to the wider community.

In a recent study of 500 Australian human resource managers[1], these cultural factors presented significant barriers to the use of telework in many organizations. Where it is used, it is often driven by a strong need to retain highly valued individuals who have difficulty travelling to work due to pregnancy, child-raising, illness or spouse relocation, or where there are difficulties in recruitment. Most arrangements are informal and not widely publicized. Despite the advantages of increased productivity, commitment, recruitment and retention, and savings on office costs shown in trials since the late 1970s (e.g. Kraut, 1987), telework is a formal part of human resources policy for only a relatively small percentage of firms.

Reasons for using telework

If corporate cultures generally present problems for telework, what sorts of organizations do adopt it? Before answering this question it is important to note that telework is used for a variety of purposes. Table 4.2 shows six motivations identified from recent survey data[1] and distinctions in the international literature (e.g. Olson, 1987; Risman and Tomaskovic-Devey, 1989). Most familiar from media publicity are high-tech organizations that manufacture computers, including Xerox, Digital, Control Data, ICL, IBM and Hewlett-Packard, and telecommunications providers, including Mercury and British Telecom, Telstra in Australia, Pacific Bell and BellCorp in the USA, and Canada's Northern Telecom. This can be related to cultural factors in the firm and industry; electronic communication is a normal part of business life, and innovation and

TABLE 4.2   Business goals and typical cultures in teleworking firms

Business orientation	Reasons for using telework	Typical culture
High-tech	ICTs are fundamental to business operations, innovation is valued	Open system Human relations
Cost reduction	To reduce office costs; replace permanent labour with cheaper, flexible contracted labour; smooth out variations in labour supply	Rational goal
Employee-centred	Employee-centred employment policies aim to maximize value of human resources	Human relations
Direct business need	To work outside office hours or to be close to clients	Rational goal
Laissez-faire	Universities and schools	Not driven by culture
Episodic	Informal arrangements are made without any strategic intention	Internal process

creativity are valued in these highly competitive and dynamic industries. The work is often project-based, with each new project requiring different patterns of networking, often amongst staff dispersed around the globe.

The smaller high-tech firms often have cultures that make telework especially acceptable. Many have flat structures and are not yet bureaucratized (Olson, 1988), despite rapid growth. Small firms may be highly dependent on a small number of highly skilled core workers, and where they live or what hours they work are less important than securing their services and commitment. As in larger high-tech firms, the information technology infrastructure is likely to be amenable but it is the culture that most influences the use of telework.

A second reason for telework is to reduce the cost of labour or to increase its flexibility (Lamond, Chapter 3). Current trends towards downsizing and re-engineering of firms indicate an increasing focus on core business and outsourcing of non-essential labour to drive down costs. Perhaps the best known example of telework for cost reduction by shedding labour is Rank Xerox's (UK) 'networking' experiment where former employees were set up as self-employed contractors (Judkins *et al.*, 1985). Another cost-cutting scenario is where full-time staff are offered telework on hourly or piece-rate pay, often with reduced benefits (Olson and Primps, 1984; Crossan and Burton, 1993). A similar rationale involves flexibility in dealing with fluctuating labour requirements, a factor behind the adoption of telework by IT manufacturer Bull (UK) (Wilson, 1991), and by a number of American IT firms (Olson and Primps, 1984). In these examples technology allows the delivery and control of work without the overheads associated with offices or standard employment conditions.

The third rationale for telework is to provide flexible employment options for staff, particularly for women with family care obligations. Although not widespread, there are organizations that have adopted telework out of a belief that greater job satisfaction, better working conditions, reduced employee travel, better work/family balance and higher commitment have business advantages, such as Pacific Bell in the USA (Christensen, 1987), UK bank Barclays (IRS, 1996) and Australian bank Westpac (Ward, 1996). A more common reason for an employee-centred approach is a shortage of skilled labour, as in the well-known case of CPS, a specific business unit set up by ICL (UK) to provide teleworking opportunities for female staff with young children (Wilson, 1991; Bailyn, 1989).

The fourth type of telework is driven by a business need to work outside office hours or in remote locations. Staff may need to interact with people or provide services outside traditional work hours, when opening a large office is expensive and commuting unattractive. Examples include brokers or agents dealing internationally, computer maintenance operations, telemarketing, telephone advisory services and emergency services. Another group work in the field, typically in sales or service occupations, and can offer greater customer service if not required to travel to a central office. The high-tech firms in the first category sometimes have similar motivations, but here telework is more tightly limited to the few staff whose work requires it. IBM (UK) is an example; telework was seen as a way to improve customer service by reducing the need for field staff to travel to head office, and as a way of providing around-the-clock responsiveness without keeping the office open (Wilson, 1991).

A fifth type of organization comprises universities and schools, which have long allowed staff to do intellectual work from home. Information and Communications technologies (ICTs) have not always been essential to this work, but now increase its effectiveness and enable a wider range of tasks to be performed remotely. Historically, the cultures of these organizations have often not required close supervision or direct control, at least for the core professional groups. The focus has been less on where work is performed than on its outcomes, especially for tasks such as research or marking that do not require personal contact.

The final type does not have a particular strategy for telework, but allows work from home on an episodic basis when, for example, a deadline is approaching or illness or child-rearing affect a staff member's ability to commute. Unlike, say, a university, telework is not part of the expected conditions of the job and management may allow it only amongst a select group, typically professionals. Clerical staff who are difficult to replace are also candidates, though less often. It may exist in only one unit that has a tolerant manager. This is the most common form of telework in terms of the number of organizations involved, though in each the number of teleworkers is small and fluctuates.

Of course, organizations do not always have a single purpose for telework. Digital (UK) is a good example, having introduced telework for three main reasons: in order to attract women and older workers who were expected to make up a larger segment of the future workforce; to meet changing aspirations in relation to career and leisure or family; and to increase operational flexibility in light of its well-developed ICT infrastructure (Wilson, 1991).

The role of occupational status

In most of the six types, cultural factors mean that certain staff are more likely to be offered telework than others, notably professional staff where they comprise a large part of the organization or hold positions of power. IT staff in high-tech firms, academics in universities and scientists in R&D organizations are good examples. These groups have high autonomy, even compared to other professionals such as accountants or lawyers who are not part of the core group of the organization. Equally, where the same professionals form a small or less valued part of the organization, telework may contravene cultural norms. In the survey mentioned above, a few mining companies had enthusiastically embraced telework for office staff, but many other firms of similar size and type of operation felt office staff should not have 'perks' unavailable to the majority of workers. It is also relevant that mining is a highly unionized industry. Similarly, in firms employing a large field-based sales or service workforce, home-based telework was not offered to professional staff. Management by output, analogous to the quota traditionally used for sales staff, was not considered because clerical staff dominated the office culture and professionals were not in a position of power.

Cultures in teleworking organizations

We have hinted at the cultures behind each type of telework, but a more systematic picture emerges if we examine theories of culture types. One useful model is Robert Quinn's Competing Values framework (Quinn, 1988), based on two sets of competing values – control vs. flexibility, and internal vs. external focus. From these Quinn identifies four prototypical cultures:

1. A *human relations* culture characterized by flexibility and an internal focus. The human relations culture is broadly oriented toward human commitment, and typically values human resources, training, cohesion and staff morale.
2. An *open systems* culture characterized by flexibility and an external focus. This culture is oriented towards expansion and adaptation to the external environment, and values adaptability, readiness, growth, resource acquisition and external support.
3. An *internal process* culture having an internal focus and a control orientation. This culture is oriented toward consolidation and continuity, and values information management, communication and stability.
4. The *rational goal* model with an external focus and control orientation. This culture aims to maximize output and values productivity, efficiency, planning and goal setting.

This typology helps to explain the relationship between the different types of telework and organizational culture (Lamond *et al.*, 1998). A *human relations* focus may favour telework as a flexible work option that will increase morale, commitment and ultimately productivity. There may be relatively little problem with giving professional or clerical employees the autonomy to work remotely, provided certain checks on past performance and self-discipline are met. A human relations focus lies behind the family-friendly and to a lesser extent the high-tech telework users.

An *open systems* orientation characterizes a growth-oriented firm in a dynamic, high-risk environment, where innovating the work process improves competitiveness. Key professionals who require sustained periods of concentration for high-quality work or high creativity may be allowed to work away from the office. Virtual teams may be seen as a way to leverage skills from widely dispersed individuals. Telework may also reduce the risk of losing key skills, by making work more attractive to women with family care obligations or individuals with certain lifestyle preferences (Bailyn, 1989). However, non-core staff, often clerical workers, may not be offered the same privileges. High-tech firms are the best examples of open systems cultures that use telework.

Telework is less likely to be used widely by *rational goal* or *internal process* cultures. Rational goal cultures use it to cover short-term staff absence, to reduce the costs of clerical labour or increase its flexibility, or where business needs dictate after-hours work or field work. Telework is not likely to be offered widely as a strategy for increasing the value of human resources. It may be seen as more appropriate to non-professional workers who can be assessed on objective work criteria, and amongst whom it can be more readily controlled. Finally, internal process cultures least favour telework because of the high value they give to rules and regulations, coordination, stability and control. Episodic telework arrangements in very bureaucratic organizations are a good example of how this common culture type uses – or limits the use of – telework.

In these ways, Quinn's model illuminates the role of culture in telework adoption. However, Quinn's archetypes are just that; few firms neatly fit into one and a typical profile involves a mix of all four even though one may have a greater role than others. When real organizations rather than archetypes were examined in a recent study[1], some broad relationships between culture and telework use emerged (Table 4.3). The most important feature was lack of emphasis on internal process, including rules and regulations, coordination, stability and control. Second in importance was a focus on productivity and accomplishment. Three other characteristics were somewhat less common but still differentiated teleworking organizations from non-users: a favourable attitude towards innovation via technology; making people feel part of the organization; and creativity and innovation. Managers seeking to implement telework will find it useful to clarify both their business goals, as listed in Table 4.2, and the extent to which their culture has the attributes shown in Table 4.3.

The impact of telework on cultures

While the issue of how culture affects telework use is important, it is also relevant to ask whether telework changes organizational culture when used over a period of years. Of course, the size of any effect would depend on the proportion of employees who telework. Although the research is in its infancy, as large-scale telework programmes are a recent development, four possibilities can be identified from the literature and recent data[1]. Telework may increase or decrease the value a culture gives to control, it may dilute the culture itself, or there may be no impact.

Formalization of control

One study of five large UK computing firms found that telework led to increased controls and more rigorous performance assessment for teleworkers

TABLE 4.3   Features of organizational cultures favouring telework

Primary characteristics	• Less emphasis on control, coordination, rules, formality, stability and predictability
	• Greater focus on productivity and achievement
Secondary characteristics	• Early adoption of technology
	• Making employees feel part of the organization
	• Creativity and innovation

(Wilson 1991), and similar results have been reported in the USA (Olson and Primps, 1984; Ramsower, 1985; Kraut, 1987). Reduced control over the immediate work process has led to formalization of control over performance generally, through such means as computerized monitoring, work fragmentation, written progress reports, regular meetings, documentation of work processes, procedures manuals, management briefing notes, specialist telework managers and increased forward planning (Wilson, 1991). Indeed, some consultants suggest that control and measurement are central to the success of telework (Gray *et al.*, 1993). Whilst some types of remote work may genuinely demand new reporting arrangements when face-to-face reporting is not available, often formalization results from the high value accorded control in many organizational cultures (Olson and Primps, 1984; Kraut, 1987; Risman and Tomaskovic-Devey, 1989). In such cases it is even possible that telework leads to formalization of control for non-teleworkers. In at least one reported case the formal methods developed to manage telework were so beneficial that they were extended right across the organization (Wilson, 1991).

Liberalizing

It might be expected that a telework programme could engender greater trust and devolution of autonomy across the organization. Bailyn (1989) suggests that by making information available and allowing rapid decisions, the technology should enhance delegation of authority, a result Bailyn found amongst some nomadic sales representatives. Research evidence of liberalization of culture is so far limited, but examples tend to involve companies where employees already have a high degree of discretion over work and are judged by overall performance, as reported for IBM (UK) by Wilson (1991). This may be either because the culture values worker autonomy or because business operations have required remote work in the past.

Diluting culture

Whatever the culture, there is a good chance that poorly implemented telework will tend to dilute it. Organizational researchers have shown how cultures are maintained by a host of symbols, statements and activities (Schein, 1990), and these are much harder to convey to distant workers. Over time, it is expected that unless specific attempts are made to include teleworkers in the culture, absence can cause them to drift away from the organization's values (Billsberry, Chapter 5). This may be particularly evident in professional teleworkers, who tend to have more allegiance to their profession, work group or product than the organization (Olson and Primps, 1984). At the same time, it is unlikely that dilution would be tolerated for a long time or where it threatened to spread widely.

No effect

Perhaps the most common effect will be none at all, simply because telework arrangements are mostly informal and small scale. Indeed, some organizations prefer to keep it that way to contain employee expectations about telework and hence disruption of organizational values (Standen, 1997).

Conclusion

Telework is not always a rational response to the capacity of technology to transform work in pursuit of greater efficiency, flexibility or employee commitment. Rather, organizational cultures hold attitudes and assumptions about the conduct of work that limit the types of innovation that will be considered, and how successful they will be. In particular, the evidence suggests that a strong emphasis on rules and procedures is a major reason many organizations do not use telework, or use it only to pursue narrow goals.

Managers planning telework are advised to consider the extent to which their work environment is focused on process, on technology as a business tool, on human relations and on achievement. While company rhetoric often stresses achievement, if processes, technology and people are managed on the basis of restrictive cultural values, achievement will be limited. This is amply shown by a study of the introduction of word-processing equipment amongst professional office workers in a variety of firms (Taylor, 1987). The most innovative and effective users of the new technology were those that had a 'systems consciousness', where the role of the innovation in the organization's larger mission was clear to managers and users. When the emphasis was on discipline and efficiency in terms of narrow output measures, the technology did not fulfil its purpose. Participation in decision making, or at least in discussions about the technology and its uses, was also an element of effective and innovative sites.

In large part, cultural factors have restricted many organizations to using telework as an informal option for a few valued individuals facing difficulties in travelling to work – not a very effective or integrative use of the technology. The biggest users today are high-tech organizations, and the greatest potential for growth appears to be amongst professionals in technologically advanced, information-based industries where innovating the work process is a business issue. Cost-cutting, meeting operational needs and retaining employees through family-friendly employment policies are other increasingly common motivations. Thus telework exists, for different reasons, in cultures with an internal or external focus, but only where flexibility is valued over control. In control-oriented cultures, telework will be seen as a stop-gap measure rather than an opportunity to adapt business systems to the external environment or to leverage maximum value from human resources.

Home-based work has been the most visible form of telework so far (Gray *et al.*, 1993; Huws, 1994), and it provides the greatest challenge to corporate cultures because home is in many ways the antithesis of an office environment (see Standen, Chapter 9). Perhaps, though, management views on trust and control of employees will evolve less in response to this radical alternative than to a wide range of less dramatic changes (Kraut, 1987) brought on by ICTs. Shared facilities can replace individual offices ('hot desking' or 'hotelling'); back offices or offshore offices can process data; travellers can work from trains, planes or remote branch offices; and staff scattered around the globe can coordinate efficiently. The growth of electronic commerce and private use of the Internet are also giving managers experience in trusting and dealing with people without face-to-face contact. It remains to be seen if this growing 'telecommunity' of business life produces corporate cultures that are less focused on internal processes.

Notes

[1]Results noted in this chapter are from a series of recent Australian studies involving teleworker interviews and surveys of human resource managers. Further details are available from the author.

References

Bailyn, L. (1989) Towards the perfect workplace. *Communications of the Association for Computing Machinery,* **32,** 460–71.

Blyton, P. (1986) *Changes in Working Time.* London: Croom Helm.

Brewster, C., Hegewisch, A. and Mayne, L. (1994) Flexible working practices: the controversy and the evidence. In C. Brewster and A. Hegewisch (eds), *Policy and Practice in European Human Resource Management.* London: Routledge.

Christensen, K. (1987) A hard day's work in the electronic cottage. *Across the Board,* April, 17–23.

Crossan, G. and Burton, F. (1993) Teleworking stereotypes: a case study. *Journal of Information Science,* **19,** 343–62.

Fierman, J. (1994) Are companies less family-friendly? *Fortune,* **129**(6), 64–7.

Gray, M., Hudson, N. and Gordon, G. (1993) *Teleworking Explained.* Chichester: Wiley.

Huws, U. (1994) *Teleworking in Britain.* Employment Gazette, February, 61–69.

IRS (1996) Turn on, tune in, churn out – a survey of teleworking. *IRS Employment Review,* **609,** 6–15.

Judkins, P., West, D. and Drew, J. (1985) *Networking in organizations: The Rank Xerox Experiment.* London: Gower.

Kraut, R.E. (1987) Predicting the use of technology: The case of telework. In R.E. Kraut (ed.), *Technology and the Transformation of White Collar Work.* Hillsdale, New Jersey: Lawrence Erlbaum and Associates.

Lamond, D.A., Standen, P. and Daniels, K. (1998) Contexts, cultures and forms of tele-working. In G. Griffin (ed.), *Management Theory and Practice: Moving to a New Era.* Melbourne: Macmillan.

McDavid, M. (1985) U.S. Army: Prototype programme for professionals. In M.H. Olson (ed.) *Office Workstations in the Home.* Washington: National Academy Press.

Nilles, J.M., Carlson, F.R., Gray, P. and Hanneman G.I. (1976) *The Telecommunications-Transportation Tradeoff: Options for Tomorrow.* New York: Wiley.

Olson, M.H. (1987) Telework: Practical experience and future prospects. In R.E. Kraut (ed.) *Technology and the Transformation of White Collar Work*, Hillsdale, NJ: Lawrence Erlbaum and Associates, pp. 135–52.

Olson, M.H. (1988) Organisational barriers to Telework. In W.B. Korte, S. Robinson, W.J. and Steinle (eds), *Telework: Present Situation and Future Development of a New Form of Work Organisation*. Germany: Empirica.

Olson, M.H. (1989) Work at home for computer professionals: current attitudes and future prospects. *Association for Computing Machinery Transaction on Office Information Systems*, **7**, 317–38.

Olson, M.H. and Primps, S. (1984) Working at home with computers: Work and nonwork issues. *Journal of Social Issues*, **40**, 97–112.

Peters, T.J. and Waterman, R.H. (1982) *In Search of Excellence*. New York: Harper and Row.

Powell, W.W. and DiMaggio, P.J. (1991) *The New Institutionalism in Organizational Analysis*. Chicago: University of Chicago Press.

Quinn, R. (1988) *Beyond Rational Management: Mastering the Paradoxes and Competing Demands of High Performance*. San Francisco: Jossey-Bass.

Ramsower, R.M. (1985) Telecommuting: The Organizational and Behavioral Effects of Working at Home. Ann Albor, Michigan: UMI Research Press.

Risman, B.J. and Tomaskovic-Devey, D. (1989) The social construction of technology: Microcomputers and the organization of work. *Business Horizons*, **32**, 71–75.

Schein, E. (1990) Organizational culture. *American Psychologist*, **45**, 109–119.

Simkin, C. and Hillage, J. (1992) Family friendly working: new hope or old hype? IMS Report No. 224. Brighton: Institute of Manpower Studies.

Standen, P. (1997) Home, work and management in the information age. *Journal of the Australian and New Zealand Academy of Management*, **3**, 1–14.

Taylor, F.W. (1911) Principles of Scientific Management. Reprinted in Taylor, F.W. (1947) *Scientific Management*. New York: Harper and Rowe.

Taylor, J. (1987) Job design and the quality of working life. In R. Kraut (ed.) *Technology and the Transformation of White Collar Work*. Hillsdale, NJ: Erlbaum.

Trist, E. (1981) *The Evolution of Socio-Technical Systems: A Conceptual Framework and Action Research Program*. Toronto: Ontario Ministry of Labour.

Ward, A. (1996) Westpac cracks the myths of home-based work. *HRMonthly*, November.

Weber, M. (1964) *The Theory of Social and Economic Organization*. London: Collier Macmillan.

Wilson, A. (1991) Teleworking – Flexibility for a few. IMS Report No. 210. Brighton: Institute of Manpower Studies.

Chapter 5

Socializing teleworkers into the organization

Jon Billsberry

How do you cope with the 'invisible' employee ? How do you ensure that the virtual worker isn't doing virtually no work at all? In this chapter, I want to look at the fit between the teleworker and the organization. In particular, I shall concentrate on the congruence of values between these two parties and discuss ways to improve this congruence. The fit between the individual and the organization is an important factor in the effective management of teleworkers because high levels of fit act as a powerful control mechanism ensuring that the 'out of sight, out of mind' employee acts in organizationally approved ways.

Some definitions

This chapter will look at ways to increase levels of person-organization fit, which means socializing people to share the values of the organization. As the terms 'values', 'socialization', and 'person-organization fit' have special meanings, they need to be defined.

'Values' are goals, standards and social principles that people hold within an organizational culture that have intrinsic worth. As Hatch says:

> They define what the members of an organization care about, such as freedom, democracy, tradition, wealth, or loyalty. Values constitute the basis for making judgements about what is right and what is wrong, which is why they are also referred to as a moral or ethical code. (1997, p. 214)

These are things that people care about; things that, if challenged, will elicit a strong response. This means that whilst values are often unspoken, they can still be identified with a little bit of effort. Values are important because they influence conscious and unconscious decision making and determine behaviour (Chatman, 1989).

Here, I shall define 'person-organization fit' as 'the congruence between the values of an individual and their employing organization'. Put simply, this means 'are the values of the individual and the organization similar?' When they are, a high level of person-organization fit is said to exist, when they are not, then there is a low level of person-organization fit. Whilst person-organization fit is a measure of how well aligned the individual and the organization are, socialization is the *process* of achieving a greater level of person-organization fit. More specifically, socialization refers to changes of values within the individual to become more like the organization. These changes can occur naturally and imperceptibly as a consequence of regular interaction with people who share other values, or the changes can occur as a result of deliberate actions by either party. Given the fundamental and enduring nature of values, socialization is a long, slow and complex process with many causes – as a result, monitoring and managing the process can be difficult.

The importance of person-organization fit

There is some debate in the literature about the importance of high levels of person-organization fit to organizations. On one side of the fence, there is concern that high levels of person-organization fit create a less diverse workforce. Schneider (1987) argues that people are attracted to the goals of the organization, are selected by the organization when they hold similar values, and choose to stay with the organization when the congruence is maintained. This cycle, termed the Attraction–Selection–Attrition (ASA) framework, explains why organizations look and feel distinctive from each other. This restriction means that employees in mature businesses are 'similar in behaviour, experiences, orientations, feelings, and reactions' (Schneider, 1987, p. 443). This can act to stifle adaptability to change or innovation and may lead to continuation of inferior work practices (Schneider, 1987; Levitt and March, 1988; Leonard-Barton, 1992).

On the other side of the fence are a group of researchers who, generally, see it as beneficial for organizations to pursue a policy of raising the level of person–organization fit. Bowen *et al.* (1991), for example, argue that in an organizational environment characterized by rapid and regular change, transition and development, recruiting 'whole people' who fit the overall organization, rather than those who fit a fixed set of task demands, is the only solution. A number of researchers (e.g. Chatman, 1991; O'Reilly *et al.*, 1991; Vancouver and Schmitt, 1991; Billsberry, 1997) have found relationships between person–organization fit and greater job satisfaction, organizational commitment, job tenure, interpersonal trust in colleagues and individual performance.

Despite these conflicting perspectives, it is possible to draw some conclusions for the specific context of teleworkers based on the underpinning arguments. In the first chapter of this book, Daniels *et al.* have developed a categorization of teleworkers. The crucial division of the classification for the analysis of person–organization fit is the intra-organizational contact dimension. Those teleworkers with high levels of intra-organizational contact, i.e. employees who regularly interact with other organizational members, are more likely to exhibit a very similar person–organizational fit profile to other employees. Of more interest are those teleworkers with low levels of intra-organizational contact, i.e. those employees who rarely interact with other organizational members. These employees are interesting because they are not subject to the same socialization processes and yet it is arguably more important that these people share the values of the organization. Why? Because of the way that values shape the behaviour of people. If remote tele-workers have a similar profile of values to the organization, i.e. they have a high level of person–organization fit, then they are likely to act in organizationally approved ways. This can be especially important for those remote teleworkers with high external contact.

Gareth Morgan (1989) suggests that organizational culture is the 'social glue' that holds everything together. We prefer to see person–organization fit as the glue; whereas the organizational culture (or organizational values) and the values of the employees are merely the two things that need bonding together. When the glue is strong, the employees naturally behave in ways the organization supports and advocates. When the glue is weak, remote tele-workers become laws unto themselves, acting in ways that might be totally contrary to what the organization would like.

Socialization

Socialization, the process of achieving person–organization fit, is a complex process of social learning involving deliberate, accidental, conscious and subconscious change within the individual. Socialization can happen whenever individuals experience something that tells them about the values of the organization. Wanous *et al.* (1984) outline the processes of socialization: coping with ambiguity, the struggle for role clarity, the identification of the organization's norms and values in early tenure, moving on to the trauma of coping with change in later organizational life. Central to all is the need to interact with the environment. This presents an intriguing problem with the socialization of distal teleworkers and very considerable problems for new teleworkers who spend much of their time situated with others not in the same organization, such as mobile teleworkers, or those at telecentres shared by several organizations. These people will almost inevitably socialize the values of those around them rather than the employing organization (this may, or may not, be desirable). Another problem concerns the limited oppor-tunities for distal workers to interact with the values of the organization. As the management of socialization is mainly concerned with the management of opportunities for people to learn about the environment, the socialization of teleworkers might seem a hopeless task. However, as I hope to demonstrate later in this chapter, this is not necessarily the case.

As one might expect, although socialization can occur at any time in an indi-vidual's tenure, socialization is greater and more rapid in the early stages of employment. When people enter organizations they want to make sense of what they have let themselves in for. Performance appraisal systems, job descriptions and procedures for managing conflict and coordination are important levers of socialization (e.g. Wanous *et al.*, 1984), aspects which are again as relevant to teleworkers as to non-teleworkers. However, socialization is a process that begins before an individual enters an organization. Socialization also occurs during the pre-entry phase of recruitment and selection – it begins the moment someone thinks about applying to an organization. Further, the initial stages of the relationship between the individual and the organization can be a period of considerable transition, but when the relationship begins to crystallize, change is much more difficult to achieve. The managerial implications are clear: *socialize employees as early as possible and don't ignore socialization opportunities during recruitment, selection or prior to entry.*

The socialization of teleworkers

Research into socialization has concentrated on the office worker, with little attention directed at teleworkers. As a result, we are left to review existing research to identify relevance for the socialization of teleworkers. The one socialization phase that is common to both teleworkers and non-teleworkers is the recruitment and selection process. This can be a most powerful socialization time because applicants are actively trying to make sense of their possible new employer. There are a number of things that employers can do to improve the likelihood of socialization during recruitment and selection.

First of all, you can change the approach to recruitment and selection (cf. Omari and Standen, Chapter 12). Most recruitment and selection textbooks use a paradigm that has remained substantially unchanged for over a hundred years. The role of the manager in this classic paradigm is to form an understanding of the job and determine the sort of person who will perform well in it. Recruitment activities then target people likely to possess the required knowledge, skills, abilities and other attributes (KSAOs). Selection activities then attempt to analyse how well each of the applicants shapes up on each KSAO and select the person who fits best. This process is set out in Figure 5.1.

Amongst the many problems with this paradigm, two stand out. First, it advocates a rationality that is very difficult to reproduce in real recruitment and selection episodes. The impression management of applicants, the limitations of selectors, the artificiality of selection situations and the poor performance of many selection techniques are just some of the reasons why selection decisions are rarely perfect. Second, it fails to appreciate the dynamics of organizational life. It is commonly said that jobs are changing more rapidly than ever before (e.g. Iles and Salaman, 1995). Changes to technology, working practices, more rapid change in the environment and so forth often mean that jobs are continually evolving to the point that new entrants commonly start jobs that are considerably different to the ones to which they were appointed. If jobs are rapidly changing and evolving to the point that they are impossible to pin down, then how can you sensibly recruit someone?

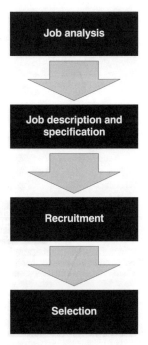

FIGURE 5.1   The classic recruitment and selection paradigm

One answer is to recruit people who share the values of the organization in addition to recruiting them because of their fit to the job. Look for people who share the values of the organization so that they can change with the organization (Bowen *et al.*, 1991) and select people who fit both the job and the organization. This new approach is reflected in Figure 5.2. It has one very important advantage for the socialization of teleworkers in so far as it minimizes the need to socialize new employees – the people taken on should already share many of the organization's values.

Whereas the assessment of person–job fit has received the attention of researchers over the past one hundred and more years, research into the measurement and assessment of person–organization fit is still in its infancy. That said, some ideas are emerging that can help select people who share the organization's values. First, you need to develop an understanding of what your organization values (cf. Standen, Chapter 4). Some artefacts, such as vision or mission statements or the Chief Executive's statement in the Annual Report, might give you an indication of some of the high-profile values. To gain a full understanding of the organization's values and how these influence employees' behaviour, however, you will need to do some more in-depth research. This can be done either through questionnaire-type surveys (e.g. O'Reilly *et al.*, 1991), or less structured techniques aimed at getting at the underlying values of the organization and how these values relate to each other and business processes (see, for example, the structured interviews outlined in Billsberry, 1996).

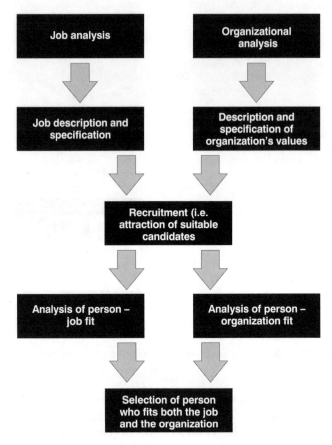

FIGURE 5.2   An emerging recruitment and selection paradigm

Once you have gained an understanding of your organization's values, you need to use the data to develop questions that you can use in an interview. The goal of the questions is to allow you to find out whether or not each applicant shares the values of the organization. At the end of every interview you should be able to say, and write down, 'I know that the first applicant has similar values to the organization because of X, Y and Z.' Obviously, you might need to phrase this negatively. As interviewing for person–organization fit might be new to you, Table 5.1 contains examples of the sort of questions that should supply you with the data you need to assess the level of person–organization fit of applicants. Clearly, you must decide which, if any, of these questions are relevant to the vacancy and each candidate. And, most importantly, you should include questions that focus on other specific characteristics of your organization's environment.

The second thing that employers can do to increase socialization during pre-entry is to develop realistic job previews. A realistic job preview is, as the name suggests, anything that gives applicants a realistic impression of what the job will be like. Basic, and rather superficial, job previews include the

TABLE 5.1   Examples of person–organization fit interview questions (from Billsberry, 1996)

1. Could you describe the social atmosphere of your previous [current] organization? [followed by] How did [does it] influence your behaviour or actions?

2. Could you compare the culture of the places where you've worked before and how the differences affected your behaviour at work?

3. You don't seem to have enjoyed working at XXXX. What was it about that company that contributed to this feeling?
[or] You seem to have enjoyed working at XXXX. What was it about that company that contributed to this feeling?

4. Where have you been happiest at work?
[followed by] What was it about the place that made you feel like this?

5. Can you describe three things that you regretted leaving behind at every company you've worked at?
[and/or] Can you describe three things that you don't regret leaving behind at every company you've worked at?

6. What do you require from an organization to get satisfaction from your work?

7. What is the attitude towards conflict [or whatever] where you currently work? [followed by] How does this fit in with your attitudes to work?

8. Why did you decide to join each of the organizations you've worked for?

9. What factors will cause you to decide whether or not to leave your current employer?

10. What do you require of an organization to perform well?

11. Try to think about when you were most unhappy at work. What contributed to this?

12. How is your effectiveness measured in your present job?

13. What factors have been important in promotions that you've gained?

14. How do you cope with working in teams [or whatever]?

15. Can you describe the characteristics and nature of your ideal organization?

16. How does your manager get the best out of you?

17. Could you describe a conducive work atmosphere for me?

18. What type of behaviour at work would raise eyebrows?

19. How will you cope with a change of employer after…years with your current company?

20. What interests you least about this organization?

'walkabout' – a guided tour around the premises – and the 'informal chat' with members of the organization who are not involved in the selection decision. A more thorough job preview should give the applicants the opportunity to find out if the job is right for them. It should give them a chance to self-select into or out of the job. Realistic job previews should give applicants an opportunity to assess for themselves what the organization will be like at a time when they are particularly sensitive to such stimuli. Commonly used methods include brochures, booklets, narrated slide presentations, oral presentations and videos. Wanous (1991) suggests six guidelines for constructing your own realistic job previews:

1. Encourage self-selection explicitly – let applicants know the purpose of the job preview.
2. The message must be credible.
3. The medium and the message must be consistent.
4. Communicate feelings as well as information.
5. Mirror organizational climates – i.e. tell people the 'good news' and the 'bad news'.
6. Do the preview early.

The 'ultimate' realistic job preview is, of course, a period of time actually doing the job. Although this is only practical in a limited number of jobs, it might have some relevance for the management of teleworkers where contracts are often short, 'zero-hour' or managed by output.

After the pre-entry phase, the next socialization opportunity is the introduction to the organization (it is useful to separate the introductory phase of the first week at work from the more general term 'induction', which refers to a more vague length of time). The introductory period needs to be managed carefully. With many teleworkers, the introductory phase might constitute the longest continuous period of time in the 'head office', and, as mentioned before, it is a time when new employees are trying to make sense of their new employer. The key to introduction is planning. Everything a newcomer encounters on the first few days, within reason, should be managed. Basics such as colleagues already knowing who the new person is, the newcomer's work environment, work assignments, and so forth, should be automatic. But the delivery of the socialization events requires more planning. The sorts of events that have proved useful for socialization include:

- many basic training activities;
- participation in teams and group work in general;
- mentoring and buddy schemes;
- experience-based approaches such as visits;
- simulations;
- role plays.

Be careful with the last two types of events as these might use artificial situations. Remember that for learning about the organization's values to occur, newcomers need to gather data about the organization upon which to reflect. When artificial data, or data about an ideal, are confronted, the effect on the newcomer is likely to be less than that when the newcomer actually experiences the organizational reality.

Two of the above-listed socialization techniques are likely to be particularly important for teleworkers with low intra-organizational contact on an ongoing basis: 'buddying' and mentoring. *Buddying* is simply pairing up the newcomer with another employee, usually someone with whom the newcomer will come into regular contact in the course of work. Ideally, the buddy should be a good role model who understands the problems that the newcomer might be facing.

The opportunity to talk to someone sympathetic, without the risk of the conversation going any further, can help newcomers understand their jobs better, help them cope with the anxiety of starting a new job, and, crucially, help them understand the subtleties of the organization better. Perhaps the best buddy is one who is already a teleworker.

A *mentor* is a person that the newcomer can approach for advice. Mentoring differs from buddying in that the mentor is usually a more experienced and more senior employee who is knowledgeable about life in the organization. Mentors are available to offer a word of advice on request, rather than the more regular help on operational matters, which is more usually associated with buddying. The power of mentoring is demonstrated by the amount of informal mentoring arrangements that spring up when there is no formal mentoring programme. It is very difficult for the teleworker with low intra-organizational contact to initiate such an informal arrangement and, conse-quently, developing a formal mentoring scheme will be a priority for many managers keen to improve the socialization of distal teleworkers.

Finally, the socialization of teleworkers is often difficult because the teleworker is thought of as a different type of worker, a worker who is somehow not core, someone who is peripheral. When such views exist, it cannot be surprising that the teleworker feels the estrangement from the organization and, as a result, does not take on the values of the organization. It can be expensive to bring in tele-workers whenever there is an office party, a talk, a briefing, a farewell, a sports day, or an anniversary to celebrate, but these are exactly the sorts of events when socialization takes place and glues together the individual and the employer.

Recommendations for management practice

By way of conclusion, we should draw together some of the ideas for socializing teleworkers that we have discussed in this chapter.

1. Change the way you look at recruitment and selection and make the assessment of person–organization fit as important as the assessment of person–job fit. Find out what the values of your organization are, and then use these as prompts for questions to identify applicants who share them.
2. Develop extensive realistic job previews for two reasons. First, they enable applicants to self-select out of jobs and organizations they don't think they will fit well. Second, they help applicants learn about the organization and its values at a time when they are inquisitive and receptive about such things.
3. Manage the introduction to work carefully so that in this key sense-making period newcomers are given every opportunity to gather data about the organization's values.
4. Consider introducing a buddying and a mentoring scheme if you don't already have one. These can greatly help the distal teleworker understand the organization and feel less remote.
5. Take advantage of every opportunity to bring remote teleworkers into the organization and treat them as you would any 'core', 'office-based' employee.

References

Billsberry, J. (1996) *Finding and Keeping the Right People*. London: Pitman.

Billsberry, J. (1997) The development and initial trial of a Likert-scaled questionnaire for the indirect assessment of person–organization value congruence. Paper presented at the Academy of Management conference, Boston, MA.

Bowen, D.E., Ledford, G.E. and Nathan, B.R. (1991) Hiring for the organization, not the job. *Academy of Management Executive*, **5**, November, 35–50.

Chatman, J.A. (1989) Improving interactional organizational research: a model of person–organization fit. *Academy of Management Review*, **14**, 333–49.

Chatman, J.A. (1991) Matching people and organizations: selection and socialization in public accounting firms. *Administrative Science Quarterly*, **36**, 459–84.

Hatch, M.J. (1997) *Organization Theory: Modern, Symbolic, and Postmodern Perspectives*. Oxford: Oxford University Press.

Iles, P.A. and Salaman, G. (1995) Recruitment, selection and assessment. In J. Storey (ed.) *Human Resource Management: A Critical Text*. London: Routledge.

Leonard-Barton, D. (1992) Core capabilities and core rigidities: a paradox in managing new product development. *Strategic Management Journal*, **13**, 111–25.

Levitt, B. and March, J.G. (1988) Organizational learning. *Annual Review of Sociology*, **14**, 319–40.

Morgan, G. (1989) *Creative Organization Theory: A Resource Book*. Newbury Park, CA: Sage.

O'Reilly, C.A., Chatman, J. and Caldwell, D.F. (1991) People and organizational culture: a profile comparison approach to assessing person-organization fit. *Academy of Management Journal*, **34**, 487–516.

Schneider, B. (1987) The people make the place. *Personnel Psychology*, **40**, 437–53.

Vancouver, J.B. and Schmitt, N.W. (1991) An exploratory examination of person-organization fit: organizational goal congruence. *Personnel Psychology*, **44**, 333–52.

Wanous, J.P. (1991) *Organizational Entry: Recruitment, Selection, Orientation, and Socialization of Newcomers* (2nd edn). Reading, MA: Addison-Wesley.

Wanous, J.P., Reichers, A.E. and Malik, S.D. (1984) Organizational socialization and group development: towards an integrative perspective. *Academy of Management Review*, **9**, 670–83.

Chapter 6

Communication and collaboration at a distance

Richard Harper

This book is testament to the fact that over the past 20 years or so, mobile communication devices and portable office technologies have afforded many new opportunities for different ways of working. These have been naturally attractive to organizations striving for commercial survival. They have allowed more flexible approaches to the spatial organization of the office, supporting both teleworking and virtual (or distributed) offices as well as more flexible working patterns (Kelly, 1985). Key to this book is the view that better implementation of teleworking processes and associated technologies can be achieved by utilizing frameworks to support decision making. What underscores this framework outlined in Chapter 1 is a concern with the behavioural aspects of telework and distributed working, rather than the technological issues.

It is behaviour that will be the focus of this chapter, too. The thesis will be put forward that, though there can be no doubt that conceptual frameworks are useful, there is always a need to recognize that each and every framework is based on various levels of detail and breadth. The applicability of any framework will be dependent upon these factors. The one offered by Daniels *et al.* (Chapter 1) has a very broad focus. We suggest that it can be supplemented by an approach to creating frameworks with greater detail, ones that more accurately reflect the organizational context to which they are to be applied. Here, we will illustrate that such frameworks help characterize how users of teleworking technologies (by which we mean anything from e-mail through to video-conferencing systems) themselves decide which technology is appropriate for their particular range of tasks. We will argue that these choices are not random or subjective, but based on recognition of organizational requirements that guide and are oriented to by members of organizations themselves.

Our argument will be illustrated with what are called ethnographically derived observational materials. In broad terms, such materials are generated by long-term observation of organizational settings, combined with what

Anderson (1997) has called an 'analytic sensibility' developed through socio-logical training. What is pertinent here is simply the fact that such an approach concerns itself with how those observed perceive and organize their own behaviour. In this case, we will report the use of two very different sorts of video-conferencing systems by a distributed work team. One type of link supported what will be called 'problem solving'. The second supported 'decision-making meetings'. We will suggest that members of the organization chose between the two systems in relationship to whether they wanted to undertake either of these activities.

We will suggest that an approach can be devised that will help explain and predict how organizational actors will make similar decisions in relation to many, if not all, of the teleworking technologies they have available, whether it be the video-conferencing systems described or any other technology. This approach is based on an understanding of how users themselves decide between different technologies and captures the detail of such decisions.

Research background

The material discussed in this chapter comes from an 18-month examination of work practices in a distributed design and manufacture centre. The purpose of this project was to determine the role of current and future teleworking technologies, with particular reference to what are sometimes called 'media spaces' or forms of real-time video connections between distributed work groups.

The work group studied was distributed across two sites, one in the UK and one in the USA. Prior to implementation of the media space technologies, the team relied mainly on telephone, fax and e-mail for communications. Distributed meetings were accomplished mainly by telephone conferencing. Documents were shared by faxing them beforehand, or by having access to electronic documents which were printed out prior to meetings.

As part of the project, two video-conferencing systems were introduced to support the work. They each had quite different characteristics. The first was 'XTV'. XTV was a fixed link, leased line video-conferencing system. Each site had a dedicated room for XTV, which encompassed large screens, document cameras and remote control facilities. The cost of the system was such that it could only be justified if it was shared with other work groups.

The second was 'MTV'. This was a mobile link that comprised a free-standing control unit with large monitor and camera. This was placed on a movable trolley and could be attached to digital phone lines in numerous rooms within both work sites. Lower costs meant that only the work group studied had rights to use this machine.

The research goal was to let the work team gradually evolve new working patterns with XTV and MTV (see also Harper and Carter, 1994). To aid in the evolution and to some degree user acceptance, we undertook some development of the technologies to make them more user friendly. This was especially the case with MTV. The ultimate goal was to use this research to deepen and contrast findings from numerous experimental and laboratory investigations into media space technologies (for media space research see Dourish and Bellotti: 1992; Gaver *et al.*, 1993; Adler and Henderson, 1994; Sellen and Harper, 1997).

Findings

It is not possible to present all the findings in great detail. But in brief, the main findings were:

- The travel budget, which had been based on previous experience, was under-spent by nearly 30 per cent at the end of a six-month trial period. Use of the video links, especially the MTV system, was cited as a significant factor in this, though because of hidden costs and other factors, this was difficult to prove conclusively.
- The two video links were used in preference to telephone conferencing for conversations amongst more than two people. In fact, telephone conferencing virtually ceased.
- The XTV system was used much less frequently than the MTV system, and only for what members of the work team themselves called more 'formal' meetings.

Thus the two systems fundamentally changed the way in which the team worked together, but there was a significant difference in the use of the two systems. Although these two systems affected a host of other technologies and associated work practices, we shall focus on the perceived differences between the two video systems.

Video and organizational action

We will start by reporting what users found preferable in each of the two systems, beginning with the issue of scheduled or *ad hoc* video conferencing.

On demand vs. pre-scheduled meetings

There was considerable difference in the two conferencing systems as regards how easily they could be brought to bear in a process.

MTV could be utilized at short notice and very flexibly. It could, quite literally, be wheeled into an office, plugged into the digital telephone sockets and a connection made (as long as the other side had also plugged in their machine!). One consequence of this was that video-conferencing meetings could and indeed often were called at very short notice. Although there was a booking procedure, open slots were usually available throughout the course of the day, and, if needed, time was found or negotiated. Thus, MTV offered something close to a dial-up on-demand system. It was these demands that drove the use of the system, rather than, say, a pre-booked session of the system demanding a meeting. Team members said that the ability to contact the remote site as and when needed was particularly useful during periods where there were urgent problems to be solved. One person pointed out that MTV was used almost constantly during critical periods.

In other words, the flexibility of calling meetings on MTV meant that distributed collaborative teamwork could be undertaken as and when needed. In this sense, MTV supported one of the important features of 'sociality' in work practice which ensures the effectiveness of work practice – namely, flexibility and adaptability (Suchman, 1987).

In contrast, XTV could only be used on a pre-booked basis – it was a shared facility only operable in certain rooms and its cost was such that fully *ad hoc* use was frowned upon. Instead, use of the system required booking in advance – sometimes days in advance. As a result, the XTV system was rarely used in response to unexpected demands, such as problems that could only be solved with discussion between members of the group on either side of the Atlantic.

However, this lack of flexibility provided XTV with a different set of advantages. One side effect of booking in advance was that it encouraged people to commit to attending a meeting. This was found to be very useful. Since staff in both sites would be involved in many meetings, one way of guaranteeing their participation was to stake a claim on their time well beforehand. This was especially important if there was a need for senior staff to attend. The result was that XTV came to be seen as more appropriate for formal management meetings than for more *ad hoc* ones.

Adherence to agenda

Users took into account the relationship between the two technologies and the completion of the agenda in a distributed meeting. More specifically, because the entire site shared the XTV facility, it was understood that XTV meetings would be scheduled around a predetermined time and consequently, an XTV-supported meeting had to finish when that time was up. Yet the fixed length of time for XTV meetings could be used to advantage, for the time limit was a useful lever in ensuring that group members adhered to an agenda. Not only was it useful in this respect, but it was also useful in forcing decisions to be made. Indeed, the strict time limit forced the participants in the distributed meetings to agree and come to a choice there and then. Of course, one way of ensuring this involved making sure that agendas for XTV meetings contained the kinds of decision issues that could be 'reasonably' decided in the time available.

In contrast, the MTV meetings varied enormously in length. As one user put it, 'they take as long as they need to take'. Even so-called process meetings, which ostensibly had strict agendas, tended to deviate away from the agenda in order to deal with specific problems or issues as they arose. In other words, MTV meetings were characterized by the fact that a large degree of business was discussed within them. When discussion took a long time, it did not result in those discussions being terminated and continued later 'offline', as has to be the case with XTV. Rather, MTV was used to get discussions 'wrapped up' within the course of the meeting (and within limits, of course).

Geographical ownership

There was one final, crucially important difference between the two systems that is worth mentioning. This gave MTV one more advantage over XTV when it came to supporting certain sorts of activities. MTV was located *within the physical environment of the work group*. This enabled access to persons, equipment and documentation as and when needed. Meetings showed a constantly changing group of people. Some members of the group would leave when the topic was no longer relevant to them, and others were brought in when their input was needed. There were also many occasions in which some document or printout was needed to address a problem. These items could be fetched quickly and used as the focus for the discussion. In other words, one characteristic of the MTV meetings was that they were dynamic in terms of people and materials, and these changes reflected the natural order of concerns in the distributed meeting.

XTV, by contrast, was deliberately located in a more 'public' place, where all work groups could get access. This resulted in there being some distance between the XTV room and the location of the offices of the work team – indeed it was a separate building elsewhere on the site. This meant that they could not easily bring in other team members or equipment and documentation if they were not anticipated prior to the meeting, especially given the time constraints of XTV meetings. Thus geographical location was one other factor which served to enforce the pre-arranged, pre-planned and more formal nature of XTV meetings.

Comment

The important point from all of this is that users of both systems started to recognize these differences as they got familiar with the systems and incorporated these 'affordances' when they chose to use one system or another. It was not simply a case of using MTV because it was convenient, for example; it was choosing MTV for certain tasks and XTV for others. Decisions as regards this related to the kinds of tasks in question. In general terms, the different tasks could be thought of as either decision making, when senior managers had to participate (XTV), or problem solving, when *ad hoc* participation was required by diverse technical and management staff (MTV).

The criteria used in deciding between technologies may be thought of as consisting of an approach that guided users' choice between different sorts of goals and tasks within a particular set of organizational and technological circumstances. The criteria were fine-grained in so far as they were closely tied to the organizational practices surrounding the use of system.

Knowledge of these practices – the need for completed decision making, for example, the requirement to bring members of the work group into MTV meetings on an *ad hoc* basis – could only be gained by looking at the context of which the systems were a part.

Table 6.1 shows a summary of the different benefits of the MTV versus XTV facilities. From this analysis it is clear that the two facilities served very different purposes for the distributed team. It shows also that the two technologies broadened the options available to the work team to support its distributed work.

Conclusion

This chapter has been primarily concerned with understanding the different ways in which video-conferencing technologies or media spaces are used within organizational contexts. Previous research into the role of such technologies had focused on what may be described as the interactional relationship between the technology and its users (i.e. the interface protocols, procedures for use, and so on). This previous research had not looked at the organizational processes the technologies were part of, such as problem solving, decision making or physical access issues that constituted the context surrounding the use of a video system (for discussion of this, see Sellen, 1997).

In the setting described here, it was found that users had a range of alternative technologies and that sometimes they selected one or other for reasons having to do with factors that were to various degrees extraneous to the technology itself. For example, it was discovered that users selected to use the XTV system as opposed to MTV system because doing so enabled them to leverage decisions more quickly. In effect, users were taking advantage of the fact that XTV meetings were subject to time constraints that MTV was not. These affordances, as we have put it, were recognized and exploited by members of the distributed work team.

One important implication of this is that the criteria used in choosing between technologies are difficult to replicate in laboratory experiments. Partly this is a matter of practical difficulties. But partly it is theoretical: the particular mix of organizational, procedural, interactional and technical

TABLE 6.1   The benefits of MTV and XTV technology

MTV	*XTV*
Supports *ad hoc* meetings	Supports formal meetings
Flexible meeting length	Fixed meeting length
Flexible agenda	Adherence to agenda
Facilitates problem solving	Facilitates speedy decision making
Access to people as needed	Secures prior commitment to attend
Access to documents and artefacts as needed	Pre-planned and pre-read documentation

concerns that influence the use and choice of one kind of technological system over another cannot be replicated in experiments since the *sine qua non* of experiment is to separate out elements of a *gestalt*, not preserve them (Harper, 1992; Sellen and Harper, 1997).

The point illustrates something of more importance in this book – that is, this research draws attention to the importance of understanding how users of teleworking technology themselves decide how best to support their distributed work. Certain technologies offer advantages over others, but these advantages may reverse themselves when a different aspect of work is at issue. Moreover, the criteria used to make such choices are often very subtle and specific to the users' context.

This has two implications. First, there is a need to understand how users develop and adapt technology within their specific organizational situations. Issues of relevance for these individuals may not be clear at the outset even to the users themselves, let alone managers and implementers of teleworking technology who may be somewhat distant from the task(s) the distributed work group wishes to undertake. There is therefore a need to undertake direct observation of the use of technology as it gets fitted into and adapted to the context in question. An approach such as that described here is one useful way of doing this.

Second, such research can lead to the development of frameworks which reflect both the level of detail appropriate for users' own decision making and the specific organizational context in question. This will be a powerful supplement to higher-level frameworks. Without such a supplement, many high-level frameworks may end up being misleading when it comes to determining what teleworking technologies are relevant or appropriate in specific, though commonplace, organizational situations. This may lead not only to false expectations but to poor implementation of strategies and design.

References

Adler, A. and Henderson, A. (1994) A room of our own: experience from a direct office-share. *In Proceedings of the ACM Conference on Human Factors in Computer Systems, (CHI '94)*, Boston, MA. New York: ACM Press.

Anderson, R.J. (1997) Work, ethnography and system design. *Encyclopaedia of Microcomputing*, **20**, 159–83.

Dourish, P. and Bellotti, V. (1992) Awareness and coordination in shared work spaces. *Proceedings of CSCW'92*, Toronto, 1–4 November.

Gaver, W.W., Moran, T., MacLean, A., Lovstrand, L., Dourish, P., Carter, K.A. and Buxton, W.B. (1992) Realizing a video environment: EuroPARC's RAVE system. In *Proceedings of ACM Conference on Human Factors in Computing Systems, (CHI 92)*. New York: ACM Press.

Harper, R.H.R. (1992) Looking at ourselves: An examination of the social organization of two research laboratories. *Proceedings of CSCW '92*, (31 Oct.–4 Nov., Toronto), New York: ACM Press.

Harper, R.H.R. and Carter, K. (1994) Keeping people apart: a research note. *Computer Supported Cooperative Work, An International Journal*, 2, 199–207.

Kelly, M.M. (1985) The next workplace revolution: telecommuting, *Supervisory Management*, **30**, 2–7.

Sellen, A. (1997) Accessing video-mediated communication: a comparison of different analytic approaches, in K. Finn, A. Sellen and S. Wilbur (eds) *Video-mediated Communication*. NJ: Erlbaum.

Sellen, A.J. and Harper, R.H.R (1997) Video in support of organizational talk. In K. Finn, A. Sellen and S. Wilbur (eds) *Video-mediated Communication*, NJ: Erlbaum.

Suchman, L. (1987) *Plans And Situated Actions: The Problem Of Human–Machine Communication*, Cambridge: Cambridge University Press.

Chapter 7

Personality and telework

David Lamond

Whether an organization has employees with the necessary knowledge, skills and abilities to do their jobs effectively depends, at least in part, on the quality of its recruitment and selection processes. When employers are looking for employees, we often hear them say 'I'm looking for the "right" person for the job' or 'I want someone with the "right" personality.' They do so because personality is an important influence on behaviours at work. This is not diminished for teleworkers.

In Chapter 1 we presented a typology of telework and sample jobs to demonstrate that there are different forms of telework and different kinds of jobs that exemplify these different forms. Is there a 'right' personality for each of these different types of telework? For example, let us say we have an employee who is effectively engaged in telework that involves off-site work with little intra-organizational and external communication (for example, data entry). Would the same person adapt as well to the form of telework that involves highly changing work, such as mobile work, with high external communication (always meeting new people) and work with high intra-organizational communication (for example, sales representative)? You might say, 'Well, obviously not.' We then have to ask the question 'Why not?'

Like so many of the issues that involve teleworking as a form of work, there is a paucity of research to guide us in answering this question. Instead, we need to rely on existing research in relation to personality and work more generally. This chapter looks to answer the question 'Is there a "right" personality for each of the different types of telework?' by examining notions of personality, its significance in relation to work behaviours, and the extent to which different personalities adapt to different forms of teleworking. Before we address the question, it is important to establish a framework within which these issues will be discussed.

As shown in Figure 7.1, work performance is the product of the interaction between individual variables – the employee's *capacity* to perform (knowledge, skills and abilities) and the employee's *willingness* to perform (motivation, attitude, personality) – and environmental variables – the *opportunity* for the employee to perform (equipment, co-workers, managers, and the organizational rules, policies and procedures) (Blumberg and Pringle, 1982). While this

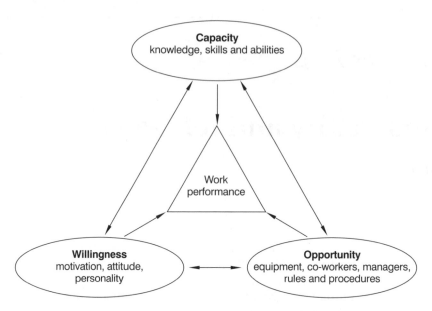

FIGURE 7.1   The relationship between individual and environmental variables, and work performance (adapted from Blumberg and Pringle, 1982)

chapter focuses on the capacity and willingness of individuals to perform, the material presented should be understood in this wider framework.

What is 'personality'?

A useful definition of personality for our purposes is that given by Statt:

> The sum total of all the factors that make an individual human being both individual and human; the thinking, feeling and behaving that all human beings have in common, and the particular characteristic pattern of these elements that makes every human being unique. (1994, p. 169)

We are talking, then, about the characteristic patterns of thinking, feeling and behaving that make individuals unique. There are many theories of personality, but two which have been given wide attention in the workplace literature are the 'Big 5' model of personality (Barrick and Mount, 1991) and the psychological type (Demarest, 1997). They represent two very different but very valuable approaches to understanding personality in the workplace. They are now considered in turn.

The 'Big 5' model of personality

This approach to personality says that personalities can be summarized or classified in terms of five basic dimensions (the 'Big 5') – extraversion, emotional stability, agreeableness, conscientiousness, and openness to experience (Barrick and Mount, 1991). The kinds of traits typically associated with each of these dimensions are listed in Table 7.1. Individuals vary in their characteristic patterns of thinking, feeling and behaviour along these different dimensions to the extent that they are more or less extraverted, emotionally stable, agreeable, conscientious and open to experience.

Psychological types

This approach aims to classify individuals according to a typology derived from their preferences in regard to how they come to know and understand the world, and how they make decisions based on that information. Developed from the work of Carl Jung (1971), this approach has been popularized through the use of the Myers–Briggs Type Indicator (Myers and McCaulley, 1985), or the MBTI as it is more commonly known. The MBTI dimensions, or preference scales, are summarized in Table 7.2. Based on individuals' scores on each of these dimensions, they are classified as one of 16 different types. For example, people who prefer to be energized by the outside world (E), who prefer to take in information indirectly through intuition (N), who prefer to make their judgements on the basis that they 'make sense' (T), and who prefer to approach life in an orderly fashion (J) would be described by the psychological type ENTJ. People who prefer to focus their attention on their inner world (I), who prefer to take in information directly through their senses (S), who prefer to make their judgements on the basis that they 'feel right' (F), and who approach life in a flexible manner (P) are described by the psychological type ISFP. These are not, however, simply types that result from E+N+T+J or I+S+F+P. Each is a unique and dynamic combination of the four dimensions into a distinctive system and ENTJs will have a very different characteristic way of thinking, feeling and behaving to ISFPs (Demarest, 1997).

TABLE 7.1 The 'Big 5' personality dimensions (adapted from Barrick and Mount, 1991)

Dimension	Characteristic traits
Extraversion	Sociable, gregarious, talkative, assertive and active
Emotional stability	Calmness, security
Agreeableness	Courteous, flexible, trusting, good-natured, cooperative, forgiving and tolerant
Conscientiousness	Dependable, organized, thorough, hard-working, achievement-oriented and persistent
Openness to experience	Imaginative, cultured, curious, original, broad-minded and artistically sensitive

TABLE 7.2   The MBTI preference scales (adapted from Demarest, 1997)

Extraversion	*Introversion*
People with a preference for extraversion focus their attention on the outer world and are energized by interaction and activity	People with a preference for introversion focus their attention on their inner world and are energized by reflection and solitude
Sensing	*Intuition*
People with a preference for sensing become aware *directly* through the five senses. They turn to and put most trust in concrete and verifiable information about what is or has been	People with a preference for intuition become aware *indirectly* through hunches, imagination and inspiration. They turn to and put most trust in flashes of insight, abstractions, theory and notions of what could be
Thinking	*Feeling*
People with a preference for thinking decide based on logic and analysis of causes and effects. For them a good decision is one that 'makes sense'	People with a preference for feeling decide based on human values and the anticipated effects of the decision on people. For them a good decision is one that 'feels right'
Judging	*Perceiving*
People with a preference for judging like to reach closure, to decide and to approach life in an orderly and structured fashion	People with a preference for perceiving like to gather information and generate alternatives, to keep their options open as long as possible and to approach life in an unstructured and flexible manner

Personality and performance

Using both these approaches to personality, researchers have been able to identify different kinds of predictive relationships between personality constructs and job-related criteria, reflecting the different approaches. Again we will examine these in turn.

The 'Big 5' model of personality

Perhaps not surprisingly, analysis of research across a range of occupational groups and job performance criteria in the USA, Canada and Europe has shown that conscientiousness is strongly related to job performance (Barrick and Mount, 1991; Salgado, 1997). Characteristics such as being persistent, careful, responsible and hardworking have been shown to be important for accomplishing work tasks in all jobs. Extraversion has been shown to be a valid predictor of performance when the work involves high levels of interaction or cooperation with others (e.g. in sales or management). Along with extraversion, openness to experience (Barrick and Mount, 1991) and conscientiousness (Behling, 1998) are related to performance in training programmes.

We might also expect those who are more open to experience to be more successful in coping with changing demands in the workplace and for learning those new and different skills. It is important to note here that the focus of this style of research has been on the relationship between personality and outcomes such as performance (assuming some common associated behavioural set) rather than between personality and the process (behaviours) by which those outcomes are achieved.

There appears to be a complex set of relationships between emotional stability and work performance (Barrick and Mount, 1991). On the other hand, a recent study by Spector *et al.* (1995) examined the possibility that individuals with certain personality traits tend to be found in certain types of jobs. They found that people who were high in trait anxiety (one of the traits associated with emotional stability) tended to be in jobs characterized by *low* autonomy, variety, identity, feedback, significance and complexity, while those who reported high levels of optimism were in jobs with *high* autonomy, variety, identity, feedback, significance and complexity.

Psychological types

Just as Spector *et al.* (1995) found a link between personality traits and job types, so research with psychological type has found that certain occupations appear to attract certain psychological types (Demarest, 1997). For example, it is estimated that, in the US population, 50–55 per cent have a preference for Extraversion, while 45–55 per cent have a preference for Thinking, 55–60 per cent for Judging and 65–70 per cent for Sensing (Demarest, 1997 p. 45). Amongst managers, administrators and supervisors though, while 51 per cent have a preference for Extraversion, 73 per cent have a preference for Thinking, 71 per cent have a preference for Judging, and only 56 per cent have a preference for Sensing (Demarest, 1997 p. 46). On the other hand, amongst marketing personnel, 67 per cent have a preference for Extraversion, 72 per cent have a preference for Thinking, 67 per cent have a preference for Judging, and only 41 per cent have a preference for Sensing (Demarest, 1997 p. 46).

Unlike the trait research, the focus of the predictions and observations about psychological type and work have centred on *how* the work is carried out – different types work at different paces, seek varying amounts of external stimulation and interaction, and communicate in different ways (Demarest, 1997 p. 53). For example, given a project that will take three days, sensing types will work at a steady pace over the three days, while intuitive types are more likely to have periods of high energy and productivity, followed by apparent lulls. Given work to do, introverts describe themselves as liking fairly long periods of time for concentration – someone or something that interferes with concentration is experienced as an interruption. On the other hand, extraverts look for something of interest in the outside world so that an 'interruption' is seen as welcome stimulation or a break. Indeed, they may go in search of stimulation and seek interaction with others. When speaking about an organization's directions for the future, those with a preference for intuition may speak of 'creating a vision' while people with a preference for sensing are more likely to talk about 'formulating goals and objectives'. In the same way, during appraisals, thinking types are likely to point out 'weaknesses', while feeling types will see 'areas for improvement' or 'opportunities for growth'.

Personality and teleworking

As we observed at the beginning of this chapter, the importance of having the 'right person for the job' is recognized in many organizations, and this is no less true for teleworking. For example, in January 1997, a report on teleworking (or telecommuting in the language of the report) was presented to the University of Michigan by its Telecommuting Task Force (Bolletino *et al.*, 1997). Among other things, the report contained a series of recommendations concerning the personal qualities that should be possessed by teleworkers. Specifically, it advocated that the employees suitable for teleworking are those who:

● are mature, self-disciplined, and capable of working with little on-site supervision;
● can demonstrate the ability to maintain productive work habits (i.e. working 8 hours per day, or the agreed amount per day or week);
● can effectively use work time to complete projects, and must be flexible;
● have strong verbal and written communication skills;
● have appropriate knowledge of the use of e-mail and faxes and other computer technology;
● have consistent, productive and organized work habits, along with the ability to make independent decisions and access appropriate technological support.

Some of the personal qualities listed by the task force are those which constitute the *capacity* of the teleworker – the knowledge, skills and abilities – to carry out the job (for example, appropriate knowledge of the use of e-mail and faxes and other computer technology). The others deal with the *willingness* of the teleworker to carry out the job (for example, by being mature, self-disciplined and capable of working with little on-site supervision). We are, of course, concerned here with the latter qualities. Before we consider the specifics of the relationship between personality and teleworking, let us return briefly to the forms of telework and the contexts within which telework takes place. In Chapter 1, we defined telework as a form of working which varies along five dimensions:

> *Location* – the amount of time spent in different locations – home, office or nomadic;
> *ICT usage* – extent of use of information and communication technologies (ICTs);
> *Knowledge intensity* – extent of knowledge required and autonomy of work;
> *Intra-organizational contact* – extent (range and intensity) of intra-organizational contact;

Extra-organizational contact – extent (range and intensity) of extra-organizational contact.

Armed with these dimensions, and our information regarding the relationships between personality and work performance, we can make some predictions about the likely relationships between personality and success in different forms of teleworking.

The 'Big 5' model of personality

The less time spent in the office, the more *self*-management becomes a critical process for getting work done. The trait characteristics associated with conscientiousness, such as being persistent, careful, responsible and hard-working, all have been shown to be important for accomplishing work tasks. These are equally applicable to the self-management involved in teleworking, where significant periods of time are spent in unsupervised work (both because of distance and the autonomy associated with high knowledge intensity work).

Also, the greater the extent of ICT usage, the more knowledge about ICTs (information and communications technologies) is required. This is, of course, a quality relating to capacity, but personality becomes an issue in regard to how that knowledge is gained. We know from previous research that, along with extraversion, openness to experience and conscientiousness are related to performance in training programmes (Barrick and Mount, 1991; Behling, 1998). From this same research, we would also expect that people who work in jobs with high levels of intra- and/or extra-organizational communication are likely to be more successful if they are higher on extraversion, agreeableness and openness to experience. Behling's (1998) concurrent finding that intelligence is positively related to work performance, while unsurprising, reminds us that intelligence is likely also to be a predictor of teleworker training outcomes in regard to success in high knowledge intensity, high ICT usage jobs.

Given the findings by Spector *et al.* (1995) in relation to trait anxiety and job type, we can speculate that those individuals with lower emotional stability are more likely to seek, be selected for or be suited to those teleworking jobs with low knowledge intensity (those with low autonomy and complexity), while those with higher levels of emotional stability would be more likely to seek, be selected for or be suited to jobs with high knowledge intensity (those with high autonomy and complexity).

Psychological types

The question of which psychological type is best suited to telework does not have a straightforward answer – it too depends on which form of teleworking you are considering. For example, you might want someone for a teleworking job where much of the time will be spent working away from the office. Using this criterion by itself, you would probably decide that you need a person with a preference for introversion – someone who prefers to work alone. If this job also involved low intra- and extra-organizational contact (for example, an information systems developer) you would be right, but if the reverse is true (high intra- and extra-organizational contact, as in the case of a sales manager), then you need a person with a preference for extraversion (note the overlap here with the 'Big 5' approach). The same complexity is true when you start to look at the four-way combinations of preferences. The key here, then, is to look at the combination of dimensions that identify the specific form of telework as a basis for deciding the appropriate type.

A detailed explication of the relationships between the hundreds of combinations of telework dimensions and the 16 personality types is beyond the scope of this chapter. However, Table 7.3 summarizes some predictions about the relationships between particular combinations of the dimensions of telework and specific personality types. In the two examples shown in Table 7.3, we see that the key difference is in the extent of the intra- and extra-organizational communication (IOC and EOC, respectively). Not surprisingly perhaps, it is the types with a preference for extraversion which are identified as more likely to be compatible with telework involving high levels of IOC and EOC, while the types with a preference for introversion are identified as more compatible with telework involving low levels of IOC and EOC. Beyond this, the extent to which high IOC involves close teamwork may determine whether the Thinking or Feeling preference combines more effectively with the preference for Extraversion. On the other hand, individuals with a preference for Perception rather than Judging are unlikely to be compatible with either of these two forms of teleworking, which demand a high degree of self-imposed goal-setting and structure.

TABLE 7.3   Personality types and telework combinations

Combination of telework dimensions	Predicted compatibility of personality types	
High ICT usage	*Compatible*	*Incompatible*
High knowledge intensity	ESTJ	ISTP
High % teleworking (high degree of autonomy)	ENTJ	ISFP
High intra-organizational communication (teamwork)	ENFJ	INTP
High extra-organizational communication		
Sample job: sales manager		
High ICT usage	*Compatible*	*Incompatible*
High knowledge intensity	ISTJ	ENFP
High % teleworking (high degree of autonomy)	ISFJ	ENTJ
Low intra-organizational communication (independent)	INTJ	ENFJ
Low extra-organizational communication		
Sample job: information systems developer		

A point about personality, teleworking and teams

Teams and team-based work systems have been recognized as the dominant organizational initiative of the past decade for enhancing the organization's ability to achieve its goals (Townsend *et al.*, 1998). We would be remiss, in this light, if we did not devote some space here to considering the implications of personality for team-based working in a teleworking context.

Two examples of research based on the 'Big 5' approach show the relationships between personality and successful team performance. In their study of product design teams, Kichuk and Wiesner (1997) found that the individuals who constituted successful teams had higher levels of extroversion and agreeableness, and lower levels of neuroticism than their unsuccessful counterparts. Thoms *et al.* (1996) used a questionnaire survey of 126 workers in a manufacturing organization that was planning the implementation of self-managed work groups. They found that emotional stability, extraversion, agreeableness and conscientiousness were significantly related to perceived self-efficacy for participating in self-managed work groups.

The psychological-type researchers also identify differences in team dynamics according to the personalities of the individuals in the teams. Demarest (1997) details some of these differences as they might show themselves during the four stages of team development – forming, norming, storming and performing. For example, during the forming stage, time is spent by team members learning about each other and forming relationships. This is an important time for those whose psychological types mean that they are people and process oriented and that they tend to do their best work when they feel a sense of relationship with their co-workers (e.g. NFs). On the other hand, those psychological types who are more task oriented and who place less emphasis on attending to group processes and forming relationships (e.g. STs) may be frustrated and want to 'get down to business'.

In their discussion about 'virtual teams', Townsend *et al.* (1998) describe the shift to 'virtual interaction' – e-mail and document sharing replace face-to-face meetings and geographic proximity, as new ways of communicating and interacting. They point out that virtual team members still need traditional teamwork – effective communication skills, goal clarity and performance orientation – but they need to learn new ways to express themselves and understand others in an environment with a 'diminished sense of presence'; they need to develop superior team participation skills, *inter alia*, because fluid membership requires quick assimilators; and they need to develop a degree of cultural sensitivity, since geographical dispersion may include national (and cultural) boundaries.

A key dynamic underpinning the virtual teams of Townsend *et al.* (1998) is the constancy of change, not only in terms of the fluidity of membership, but also in the way they transcend traditional fixed functional roles and carry out a changing variety of assignments and tasks. We should, therefore, also explore the capacity of our teleworkers to adapt to that kind of change. From the perspective of the 'Big 5', we know that extraverts and those who are more open to experience are more likely to adapt successfully to these kinds of changing circumstances (Barrick and Mount, 1991; Salgado, 1997). We would therefore be keen to ensure that the members of our team score high on these traits.

Differences in the posture of the different psychological types to organizational change have also been identified (Demarest, 1997). Some of these broad differences are summarized in Table 7.4. One of the differences between the sensing types ('Let's keep things as they are') and the intuitive types ('Let's change things') is the result of the sensing types wanting data or experience to support the new direction, while the intuitive types are comfortable proceeding based on a general idea or a hunch. On this basis, in the language of psychological type, we would be looking to populate our teams with Ns rather than Ss. Similarly, those with preference for extraversion are action oriented and want to move ahead more quickly, while those with a preference for introversion move ahead more slowly, wanting time to reflect.

Conclusion

Clearly, there are particular forms of teleworking and teleworking contexts that individuals will find more or less stimulating and to which they will be more or less suited. When making our selection decisions, we are not just talking about individuals or the jobs we want them to do; we are talking about the 'goodness of fit' between those individuals and their jobs (Billsberry, Chapter 5). The more people feel that their jobs are stimulating, rewarding and challenging, the more they will respond with their best efforts and creativity (they will be satisfied and productive); the more they feel their job is stultifying or beyond their capabilities or interests, the more dissatisfied and unproductive they will be (Statt, 1994 p. 101). We are looking less for the 'right' person for our teleworking job, than we are for the right 'match' between the person and the job. Table 7.5 summarizes the expected relationships between the personality traits and types and the dimensions of telework, based on the earlier discussion.

Teleworkers, like all workers, need to be conscientious, but perhaps need, to a greater extent, to be self-reliant and self-motivated. They also need to be disposed towards the different co-worker and supervisory relationships and different communication patterns that off-site work requires. Telework, of itself and in its different forms, will not, therefore, suit all workers equally. It behoves us to ensure that we use our insights to get a match between the right person and the right teleworking job.

TABLE 7.4 Psychological type and postures to change (adapted from Demarest, 1997)

Introversion Sensing (IS)	*Introversion Intuition (IN)*
'Let's keep things as they are'	'Let's look at this another way'
Extraversion Sensing (ES)	*Extraversion Intuition (EN)*
'Let's get on with it'	'Let's change things'

TABLE 7.5   Personality traits, types and their links to dimensions of telework

Telework dimension	Personality traits	Personality type dimensions
Information and communication technology	Openness to experience	Sensing–Intuition Introversion–Extraversion
Knowledge intensity	Emotional stability	Sensing–Intuition
Location	Conscientiousness	Introversion–Extraversion Judging–Perceiving
Intra-organizational communication	Extraversion, agreeableness, openness to experience	Introversion–Extraversion Thinking–Feeling
Extra-organizational communication	Extraversion, agreeableness, openness to experience	Introversion–Extraversion Thinking–Feeling

References

Barrick, M.R. and Mount, M.K. (1991) The big five personality dimensions and job performance. *Personnel Psychology*, **44**, 1–26.

Belling, O. (1998) Employee selection: will intelligence and conscientiousness do the job? *Academy of Management Executive*, **12**, 77–86.

Blumberg, M. and Pringle, C.D. (1982) The missing opportunity in organizational research: some implications for a theory of work performance. *Academy of Management Review*, **7**, 560–7.

Bolletino, L., de Pietro, L., Kari Gluski, K., Lauerman, E., Leacock, G., Lebowitz, L., Martin, N., Ostron, D., Rojo, L. and Steiner, C. (1997) ITD Telecommuting Task Force Report. University of Michigan: http://www.itd.umich.edu/telecommuting/report/index.html.

Demarest, L. (1997) *Looking at Type in the Workplace*. Gainesville, FL: Center for Applications of Psychological Type.

Jung, C.G. (1971) *Psychological Types* (trans H.G. Baynes; rev R.F.C. Hull). London: Routledge.

Kichuk, S.L. and Wiesner, W.H. (1997) The big five personality factors and team performance: implications for selecting successful product design teams. *Journal of Engineering and Technology Management*, **14**, 195–221.

Myers, I.B. and McCaulley, M.H. (1985) *Manual: A Guide to the Development and Use of the Myers–Briggs Type Indicator*. Paolo Alto, CA: Consulting Psychologists Press.

Salgado J.F. (1997) The five factor model of personality and job performance in the European community. *Journal of Applied Psychology*, **82**, 30–43.

Spector, P.E., Jex, S.M. and Chen, P.Y. (1995) Relations of incumbent affect-related personality traits with incumbent and objective measures of characteristics of jobs. *Journal of Organizational Behavior*, **16**, 59–65.

Statt, D.A. (1994) *Psychology and the World of Work*. London: Macmillan.

Thoms, P., Moore, K.S. and Scott, K.S. (1996) The relationship between self-efficacy for participating in self-managed work groups and the big five personality dimensions. *Journal of Organizational Behavior*, **17**, 349–62.

Townsend, A.M., DeMarie, S. and Hendrickson, A.R. (1998) Virtual teams: technology and the workplace of the future. *Academy of Management Executive*, **12**, August, 17–29.

Chapter 8

Job features and well-being

Kevin Daniels

The purpose of this chapter is to examine the factors that influence the well-being of teleworkers. For the most part, we concentrate on psychological well-being, although we will examine some of the risks to physical well-being. We concentrate on psychological well-being for two reasons. First, there are demonstrable relationships between poor psychological well-being and poor physical health, for example cardiovascular disease (Daniels, 1992). Second, there are significant associations between psychological well-being and a range of behaviours associated with performance and productivity – such as absenteeism – and commitment to the organization (e.g. Brooke and Price, 1989; Wright *et al.*, 1993; Van Dyne *et al.*, 1994). Management and systems that enhance psychological well-being can have important organizational and individual benefits.

The major elements of psychological well-being are healthy mental and social functioning. Perhaps the most central element is the experience of positive emotions, together with infrequent experience of negative emotions. Such positive emotions include happiness, joy, optimism, relaxation and being active. Amongst the negative emotions are anxiety, depression, sadness, boredom, anger and fatigue (see Daniels *et al.*, 1997). Other components of well-being also include satisfaction with life or work, self-esteem, positive relations with others and a feeling of being in control (e.g. Ryff and Keyes, 1995).

Psychological well-being is domain specific (Warr, 1990), that is, people have different levels of well-being for different life areas, such as work and family. Clearly, these are related – someone with poor well-being at work is likely to have poor well-being out of work. Nevertheless, well-being is to some extent specific to each context. In this chapter then, we are concerned with psychological well-being in the work domain. Most of the chapter examines the job features associated with well-being and how teleworking might affect these job features. We also examine preventative strategies for maintaining desirable job features.

Job features and well-being

Warr (1994) has described the features of psychologically healthy jobs. These are:

1. *Opportunity for control.* This applies to autonomy over the job itself and the opportunity to participate in decisions affecting the wider work context. Usually, opportunity for control enhances well-being. However, jobs with excessive opportunity for control, especially those which are also associated with extreme responsibility, could cause poor well-being.
2. *Opportunity for skill use.* Workers who are able to use their full range of skills and knowledge often experience greater psychological well-being. Of course, jobs can cause poor well-being if they require skills that workers do not have.
3. *Variety at work.* If there is little variety at work, then the work is boring and becomes of a cause of poor well-being. If there is too much variety, then work can become fragmented.
4. *Work demands.* This applies to both physical and mental demands, as well as the pace and difficulty of the job. Jobs with excessive intellectual demands, physical demands or time pressures can be a cause of poor well-being. Jobs with very few demands usually are associated with low job control, low use of skills and little variety, often making these jobs a cause of poor well-being too. Jobs with balanced demands are often the best for well-being.
5. *Job and organizational clarity.* This is information about job roles. It subsumes ambiguity about current job roles, future job roles and future job security. Clarity is important for well-being, provided the rules, procedures and regulations that can help ensure clarity do not compromise flexibility and discretion.
6. *Availability of money.* This includes low absolute wages and lower wages relative to others in the same organization or job.
7. *Good physical working conditions.* Very noisy, hot, cold, wet, physically threatening or poorly designed work environments can cause poor psychological and physical well-being.
8. *Social contact and interpersonal support.* Social contact and supportive work environments can help offset poor well-being caused by other job features. Support can come from supervisors, co-workers and from non-work sources such as family and friends. Nevertheless, many people do require some privacy for some tasks – and too much social contact can become annoying or distressing.
9. *Valued social position.* A valued position, whether in society as a whole or within an organization, can be a cause of greater well-being. Jobs with low social status can be associated with poor well-being. Career development factors (Cooper and Marshall, 1976) are also relevant to this job characteristic, in that individuals that have been under-promoted or have fewer career opportunities are unlikely to feel that others in the organization value them.

In general then, psychologically healthy jobs feature adequate amounts of control, variety, skill use, clarity and social contact and support. They are also characterized by balanced work demands, good physical working conditions, appropriate payment and a valued position in the organization.

Job features and telework

Despite different forms of teleworking, all teleworkers share remoteness from other organizational members. For this reason, all forms of teleworking can influence some job features in the same way (Standen *et al.*, 1999). Nevertheless the factors used to differentiate forms of teleworking listed in Chapter 1 here can have very specific effects on job features.

Opportunity for control

Autonomy over content and scheduling of work tasks: Standen *et al.* (1999) consider that electronic monitoring of output is easier for lower knowledge intensity clerical work, such as data entry – and electronic surveillance is less flexible than direct supervision. For this reason, Standen *et al.* (1999) consider that teleworking could lower the autonomy experienced by low knowledge-intensity teleworkers. Electronic monitoring is almost impossible for high knowledge-intensity teleworkers. This could help enhance the autonomy of high knowledge intensity teleworkers based at home or in a satellite office. Autonomy might also be greater for knowledge-intensive mobile teleworkers, who by the nature of their work can be less easy to contact (Daniels, 1999). Even if tasks cannot be changed to allow greater autonomy and discretion, all teleworkers could be allowed to schedule their work tasks. This would mean agreeing targets to be achieved by a given time – but would enable at least some autonomy over work, and allow more opportunities to integrate the demands of work and non-work life (see Standen, Chapter 9).

Participation in decision making: We might expect remote working to lessen the chances of participation in decisions. Provided steps are taken to ensure adequate social contact within the organization (see below), teleworkers should be able to participate in decisions. For example, Daniels (1999) found that teleworkers who visited the main office site for a few days per week did not report any less opportunity to participate than office workers in similar jobs. Nevertheless, it is important for teleworkers to realize that they can participate in decisions – and managers should encourage teleworkers to do so. Teleworkers who have a lot of extra-organizational communication, especially in high knowledge intensity work, may find that contact with customers or suppliers gives access to information that other workers, and even managers, do not have (Daniels, 1999). In these circumstances, we might expect to find that such workers have many opportunities to participate in decisions at work.

Opportunity for skill use

For people such as those who are disabled or those caring for children, elders or ill relatives who could not engage in traditional work, teleworking allows access to employment (Haddon, 1991). In this sense, it can provide an opportunity for skill use, particularly for professional workers (Standen *et al.*, 1999). For low knowledge intensity workers, skill use may be curtailed through management by outputs. Two strategies may help here – ensuring rotation across different job tasks, and enriching opportunities for discretion and autonomy over tasks to enable greater influence over decisions.

Variety at work

Gillespie *et al.* (1995) indicated that teleworking may lead to increased routinization of tasks, lessening control, skill use and especially variety of tasks. For low knowledge intensity home and satellite office workers, this is a salient danger (Standen *et al.*, 1999). For mobile teleworkers, there is evidence of an increase in variety at work, as the worker moves from one place to the next (Daniels, 1999). As for skill use, rotation through tasks and enriching discretion over tasks may provide a solution for those at risk.

Balanced work demands

There have been reports of home-based teleworkers working longer hours (Tucknutt *et al.*, 1995) and mobile teleworkers reporting greater work demands (Daniels, 1999). Further, where the work requires extensive contact with others and there are many channels of communication open (e-mail, telephone, fax), teleworkers may experience 'information overload' (Sparrow, 1998) or conflicting demands from many different stakeholders (Daniels, 1999). Also, technical problems can increase the difficulty and time pressure of work. Conversely, home-based teleworking especially can allow greater flexibility to work the hours when the worker is most productive and to avoid interruptions (Standen *et al.*, 1999).

The evidence indicates that excessive work demands can be a problem. One solution might be for teleworkers and managers to establish a realistic diary of routines and tasks (Ingham, 1995) and include time management and prioritization as part of training and development for teleworkers. Information technology that allows teleworkers access to information remotely may enable teleworkers to obtain the information in a timely manner to reduce workload. To avoid problems of information overload, the technology must allow teleworkers to prioritize incoming messages.

Job and organizational clarity

Telecommunications are unlikely to substitute for face-to-face contact in terms of body language, vocal tone, the reactions of others and informal networks

(Shamir and Salomon, 1985). As such, teleworkers often report a reduction in quality and quantity of information, especially that related to performance feedback, organizational politics and organizational strategy (Crossan and Burton, 1993). In a satellite office with a significant number of people from the same organization, the problems may not be as great. The most successful tele-working schemes have clear goals and objectives for teleworkers, which help to provide greater role clarity and the chance for teleworkers to gauge their performance against their objectives (Cox *et al.*, 1996). Cox *et al.* (1996) have also suggested implementing reporting systems, even where managers do not think they are necessary, as these can provide informal information networks. Establishing communication channels amongst co-workers, provided they do not lead to information overload, can also provide information networks. Scheduled telephone calls or informal e-mail exchange are two possibilities. Where possible, encouraging people to visit the office for a few days a week can provide perhaps the best access to informal networks (cf. Daniels, 1999).

Availability of money

In some low knowledge intensity clerical jobs, teleworking is associated with less pay and payment by outputs (Huws, 1994). However, because of savings from reduced commuting, lunches and clothing (Haddon and Lewis, 1994), home-based teleworkers especially should report better pay adequacy. This effect may be especially noticeable for those that would otherwise have to commute long distances. However, organizations should ensure that tele-workers' pay is at least comparable to traditional workers performing similar work, as relative pay is at least as important as absolute pay.

Good physical working conditions

Huws (1994) reports an Institute of Personnel Management survey in which 42 per cent of a sample of teleworkers reported eyestrain, 28 per cent backache and 20 per cent neck pain. Only 14 per cent of the sample reported no physical health complaints. Low knowledge-intensity teleworkers may experience even more problems than this, as they are more likely to do monotonous and repetitive display screen work (Cox *et al.*, 1996). For teleworkers, physical problems could be caused by cramped surroundings, static working condi-tions, unsuitable furniture, poor lighting, poor ventilation and VDU glare (Cox *et al.*, 1996). Such poor working conditions can also affect psychological health.

For home-based teleworkers, possible solutions include having a designated room for working and the payment of allowances to buy suitable furniture and adapt premises for teleworking (Huws, 1994). A designated room is more likely to establish boundaries between work and home, and act to prevent spillover of work problems into the home environment (see Daniels, 1999; Standen, Chapter 9). Higher paid, high knowledge-intensity workers may establish a designated work space more easily, but they are also least likely to be at risk from ergonomic problems anyway (Cox *et al.*, 1996). The best approach is to manage the physical risks of teleworkers in the same way as traditional workers. Employers should:

- with prior arrangement, visit the premises;
- ensure that the workplace complies with Health and Safety legislation;
- ensure that furniture and equipment are suitable for the work;
- ensure that there is sufficient ventilation, lighting, and VDU glare is limited;
- ensure that there is suitable storage for equipment when not in use;
- ensure that there are procedures for reporting accidents and hazards;
- ensure that the worker is insured (European Community legislation grants homeworkers the same rights at home as in a traditional work place);
- ensure that the worker understands the personal relevance of Health and Safety legislation;
- ensure that the worker understands the importance of taking rest breaks, and that the worker is able to do so;
- ensure that the worker understands the nature of the insurance cover;
- advise the other occupants about the equipment;
- ensure that the worker keeps children, pets etc. away from the equipment.

(adapted from Gray *et al.*, 1993)

Many items in this checklist are most readily applied to home and satellite office workers, or to mobile workers with a limited set of work locations. All teleworkers should receive health and safety training to avoid physical problems. This training is especially important for mobile teleworkers who often have to adapt to changing locations to perform tasks.

Social contact and interpersonal support

Social isolation is one factor that is commonly mentioned in relation to teleworking (Gray *et al.*, 1993, Gillespie *et al.*, 1995), and is most likely amongst home-based teleworkers, and teleworkers with little intra- or extra-organizational contact. In interviews conducted with teleworkers we have found that support helps teleworkers considerably in managing their work problems. Support from friends and family can help teleworkers emotionally, but support from colleagues, supervisors and technical experts also provides the tangible assistance to solve work and technical problems. Establishing support networks is very important for teleworkers. For non-technical support, some evidence indicates that visiting the main office for a few days a week can be sufficient to prevent problems (Daniels, 1999). Like job and organizational clarity, establishing reporting relationships and communication channels could enhance contact and support (see above). Making teleworkers feel part of the organization may also help, through socialization activities (see Billsberry, Chapter 5) and social events with co-workers. Notwithstanding such strategies, it is especially important to establish efficient and readily available technical and managerial support.

Valued social position

Teleworkers lose visibility in the main office, and teleworkers may feel they are valued less than non-teleworking colleagues (Standen *et al.*, 1999) and that they (teleworkers) have reduced opportunities for promotion (Gillespie *et al.*, 1995). Reduced social value and opportunities for promotion may be more salient for high knowledge-intensity workers socialized towards these issues (Standen *et al.*, 1999). Conversely, as low knowledge-intensity teleworkers are often managed by outputs, this may indicate a lack of trust from management (Huws, 1993) and therefore lowered social standing. However, reduced career opportunities do not appear to be a problem for high knowledge-intensity teleworkers that regularly communicate with customers and suppliers (Daniels, 1999). It is possible that such workers are able to broker the information obtained through their boundary-spanning activities to negotiate better career progression. For other teleworkers, however, there are a number of possible interventions. Techniques for reducing isolation (see above) can help establish visibility. Teleworkers could also receive encouragement from managers and training to enhance visibility, especially by using IT. As well as establishing more frequent reporting, establishing regular career development meetings with line managers can enhance the perception of value and that the organization treats teleworkers' careers seriously.

Conclusion

Organizations have a clear ethical responsibility to ensure the psychological and physical well-being of teleworkers (Moon and Stanworth, 1997). In addition, as outlined earlier, enhancing well-being could provide benefits for performance and commitment.

Table 8.1 summarizes the risk factors associated with telework and possible interventions. These interventions are preventative, and targeted at specific job features. Strategies aimed at enhancing performance may also have beneficial effects for well-being. Enhancing teleworking competencies through training or selection may also provide teleworkers with the skills to elicit support effectively, deal with technical problems etc. (see Omari and Standen, Chapter 12; Salmon *et al.*, Chapter 14). Teleworking managers too should be selected and trained to be sensitive to specific teleworking issues. Distance learning packages aimed specifically at enhancing coping skills in teleworkers, teleworking support networks and remote counselling provision for teleworkers are developments that need to become widely accessible to help manage teleworkers' well-being, and could provide useful additions to preventative interventions aimed at job features.

Any intervention should begin with some assessment of existing job features and their relationship to well-being (Daniels, 1996). In so doing, a picture emerges of which job features need to be enhanced, and whether any particular groups are at particular risk. This assessment forms the basis of a well-informed intervention. There are many widely available measures of job

TABLE 8.1 Job features, risk factors and interventions

Job feature		Risk factors	Interventions
Low control	autonomy	Low KI	Discretion and autonomy – especially scheduling
	participation	All except high EOC + high KI	frequent visits to main office, encouraging teleworker participation
Low skill use		Low KI	Task rotation, discretion and autonomy
Low variety		Low KI + home or satellite	Task rotation, discretion and autonomy
High demands		Home, mobile, high IOC, high EOC, ICT use	Diary of routines and tasks; time management/prioritization training; ICT to help prioritize incoming messages
Low job and organizational clarity		All	Clear goals and objectives; reporting systems; communication channels amongst co-workers; frequent visits to main office
Low wages		Low KI	Pay comparable to traditional workers in similar jobs
Poor physical working conditions		All, especially low KI	Allowances for suitable furniture and to adapt premises; designated room for working; inspect premises; health and safety training
Low social contact/support		All, especially home, low IOC, low EOC	Reporting systems and communication channels; socialization activities; social events; frequent visits to main office; technical and managerial support.
Low social value		All, except high EOC	Enhance support and contact; establish visibility in organization; career development meetings

Key: KI = knowledge intensity; IOC = intra-organizational communication; EOC = extra-organizational communication features, well-being and coping skills, but these have been developed for traditional office work in the main. For teleworkers especially, it could be important also to assess job features, and their relationship to non-work life. Perhaps more than for any other group of workers, the relationship between work and non-work is salient for teleworkers. Standen addresses these in the next chapter. Awareness of the issues in totality is important.

References

Brooke, P.P. and Price, J.L. (1989) The determinants of employee absenteeism: an empirical test of a causal model. *Journal of Occupational Psychology*, **62**, 1–19.

Cooper, C.L. and Marshall, J. (1976) Occupational sources of stress: a review of the literature relating to coronary heart disease and mental ill health. *Journal of Occupational Psychology*, **49**, 11–28.

Cox, T., Griffiths, A. and Barker, M.J. (1996) *Teleworking: Health and Safety Issues in the Members States of the European Union*. Dublin: European Foundation for the Improvement of Living and Working Conditions.

Crossan G. and Burton, F. (1993) Teleworking stereotypes: A case study. *Journal of Information Science*, **19**, 343–62.

Daniels, K. (1992) *Occupational Stress and Control: Implications for Employee Well-Being*. PhD thesis, Cranfield University.

Daniels. K. (1996) Understanding stress and stress management. In R. Paton, G. Clark, G. Jones, J. Lewis and P. Quintas (eds) *The New Management Reader*. London: Routledge.

Daniels, K. (1999) Home based teleworking and mobile teleworking: a study of job characteristics, well-being and negative carry-over. *Work Science Report Series*, 13/14, 1535–6. Tokyo: Institute of Science of Labour.

Daniels, K., Brough, P., Guppy, A., Peters-Bean, K.M. and Weatherstone, L. (1997) A note on a modification to Warr's measures of affective well-being at work. *Journal of Occupational and Organizational Psychology*, **70**, 129–38.

Gillespie, A.E., Richardson, R. and Cornford, J. (1995) *Review of Teleworking in Britain: Implications for Public Policy*. London: Report to the Parliamentary Office of Science and Technology.

Gray, M., Hodson, N. and Gordon, G. (1993) *Teleworking Explained*. Chichester: Wiley.

Haddon, L. (1991) Disability and Telework. Ipswich: BT Laboratories, Martlesham Heath.

Haddon, L. and Lewis, A. (1994) The experience of teleworking: an annotated review. *International Journal of Human Resource Management*, **5**, 193–223.

Huws, U. (1993) *Teleworking in Britain: A Report to the Employment Department*. London: Employment Department Research Series.

Huws, U. (1994) *Teleworking*. Brussels: European Commission's Employment Task Force (Directorate General V).

Ingham, C. (1995) *Working Well at Home*. London: Thorsons.

Moon, C. and Stanworth, C. (1997) Ethical issues in teleworking. *Business Ethics: A European Review*, **6**, 35–45.

Ryff, C.D. and Keyes, C.L.M. (1995) The structure of psychological well-being revisited. *Journal of Personality and Social Psychology*, **69**, 719–27.

Shamir, B. and Salomon, I. (1985) Work-at-home and the quality of working life. *Academy of Management Review*, **10**, 455–64.

Sparrow, P.R. (1998) Information overload. In K. Legge, C. Clegg and S. Walsh (eds) *The Experience of Managing: A Skills Workbook.* London: MacMillan.

Standen, P., Daniels, K. and Lamond, D. (1999) The psychological well-being of teleworkers: a theoretical framework. Working Paper, Perth: Edith Cowan University.

Tucknutt, D., Griggs, J. and Maternaghan, M. (1995) Teleworking Trial. Ipswich: BT Laboratories, Martlesham Heath.

Van Dyne, L., Graham, J.W. and Dienesch, R.M. (1994) Organizational citizenship behavior: construct redefinition, measurement, and validation. *Academy of Management Journal,* **37**, 765–802.

Warr, P. (1990) The measurement of well-being and other aspects of mental health. *Journal of Occupational Psychology,* **63**, 193–210.

Warr, P. (1994) A conceptual framework for the study of work and mental health. *Work and Stress,* **8**, 84–97.

Wright, T.A., Bonnett, D.G. and Sweeney, D.A. (1993) Mental health and work performance: results of a longitudinal field study. *Journal of Occupational and Organizational Psychology,* **66**, 277–84.

Chapter 9

The home/work interface

Peter Standen

Work at home is not only the most common form of telework but also the one that differs most from traditional work practices. From another perspective, though, moving work into the home goes 'back to the future', as most work was conducted at or near home before the industrial revolution. Indeed, since Toffler (1980), futurists have foreseen the computer revolution returning us to a more harmonious, decentralized society based around the 'electronic cottage'. However, working life and home life today are considerably different to what they were even 20 years ago. Working hours are longer and jobs more demanding, family life is subject to new pressures, and concern over work/family balance is growing (Zedeck and Mosier, 1990; Lewis and Cooper, 1995). These pressures create challenges for work at home but at the same time make it more attractive to many workers. In this chapter we consider how teleworkers and their managers can minimize the problems and maximize the benefits of this reinvented mode of work.

Some of the problems are known from research in the 1980s (Brief, 1985; Shamir and Salomon, 1985; Kraut 1987). Home-based telework contravenes many of the premises on which modern organizations are built, including face-to-face communication, continuous monitoring of workers, the use of organizational culture and social events to motivate and influence workers, standardized working hours, a business-like environment, and the strict separation of work from private life. Some of the resulting issues are common to all forms of telework, and are dealt with elsewhere in this book. At the same time, work at home can have very different hours, social influences and physical conditions to work in conventional offices or other forms of telework. The potential for disruptions by family members, distraction by domestic or leisure options, poor physical conditions and difficulties in managing the different schedules of work and home life led the early researchers to conclude that work at home would not be viable for large numbers of workers. These issues are the focus of this chapter.

More recent research[1] shows that while work at home is not as convenient as Toffler suggests, with appropriate management, worker skills and family circumstances it does not need to be problematic. Home-based workers are often satisfied with the arrangement and more productive than office workers (Olson, 1987; Leidner, 1988; Hartman *et al.*, 1991). However, success in telework depends on managers and workers understanding its unique nature.

Figure 9.1 shows the key influences on work at home, including the organization, the family or other co-residents, the community, the physical conditions of the work site and the time schedules of work and non-work life. Perhaps the major theme from the research is the importance of creating a boundary between work and home life to reduce the *'spillover'* between them. Other important factors include autonomy in work and family life, the social value of work at home, equity issues and social contact. Decades of research show that these factors affect performance, satisfaction and well-being in conventional workers (Hackman and Oldham, 1980; Greenhaus and Beuttell, 1985; Warr, 1987), and in home-based telework they should not be taken for granted.

FIGURE 9.1   The home/work interface.

Family and work: spillover and compensation

In many ways modern society has evolved to keep work and home life separate. At work, social conventions, organizational cultures, management styles – even furnishings and attire – act to keep workers focused on work roles. Conversely the home is not designed for work and families often resent work intruding into it. However, work and family roles are not fully compartmentalized even in conventional work: people think about home life at work, and vice versa, and every so often one interrupts the other. This spillover is likely to be greater when work and home life exist in the same place: roles are more easily switched, intrusions are more likely and mental disengagement is harder. Spillover can occur even when family members are not present during work.

An indication of the importance of switching roles comes from studies which show how commuting, for all its drawbacks, provides an important opportunity mentally to switch roles. Home-based workers use a wide range of 'transition rituals', including exercise, grooming or dressing, meditation and even housework to take its place (Ahrentzen, 1990). It is likely that similar strategies are used to unwind from work and re-enter family roles. Even those who can just walk into the office and start work will have mental strategies for keeping their attention on work during the day.

The importance of separating work and home life is also shown by studies of how negative emotions spillover in conventional work, such as when frustrations from work lead to increased family friction (e.g. Greenhaus and Beutell, 1985). At work, spillover produces stress and dissatisfaction and may be a factor in poor productivity and health problems (Zedeck and Mosier, 1990). At home, it can affect family life by reducing communication, creating parent–child conflict, increasing the monitoring of children, changing family roles and restricting household use (Leidner, 1988; Ahrentzen, 1990; Gurstein, 1991). Worse, these problems can 'spill back' and compound the original problem. It is therefore important that teleworkers are able to set boundaries between work and home life, and the support of family members will be needed to do this.

On the other hand, many individuals seek telework to balance the time demands of work and family life. Parents of young children are a major group in home-based telework, and it appears that most are satisfied with the arrangement. Even if, as widely recommended, they do not look after children while working, telework gives better access to schools, care facilities, shops and other essential resources. For similar reasons, elder care is a growing reason for seeking telework. Some spillover may still occur where workers have family care obligations, but with appropriate management it is probably less than in a distant office, bringing better work outcomes and greater satisfaction with family life.

Home life and work life also have a *compensatory* relationship when problems in one area lead to increased effort in the other (Lambert, 1990). For example, failure to achieve career goals leads some to take up hobbies or invest greater time in family life. In general, separating work and family life probably helps compensation, suggesting a problem for teleworkers. Possibly, though, small forms of compensation occur more often in telework: a problem at work may lead to a temporary switch to something more rewarding. Despite this, there is evidence that having multiple roles in life benefits one's self-esteem and well-being (Sieber, 1974), and these may be jeopardized if home-based work reduces variety in activities, social contact, sources of social value or sources of self-identity (e.g. Brief, 1985; Shamir and Salomon, 1985). This means that home-based teleworkers may need to find other outlets – such as the local community or sporting clubs – to compensate for loss of variety in life roles.

Greater spillover and reduced compensation are a function of the boundary between work and home life, to which we now turn.

Setting a boundary between work and other activities

The boundary between work and family or community may be physical (a separate room), temporal (working when others are not present) or social (people are asked to respect the worker's privacy). As much as anything else, though, the boundary is psychological (Ahrentzen, 1990; Gurstein, 1990): one must be able mentally to disengage the work and other roles.

Physical boundaries

A home work site generally needs to be physically separate from the rest of the house, particularly for work that requires a great deal of concentration; indeed, tasks with low intellectual content may actually be more pleasant in the presence of suitable distractions. Physical separation not only keeps out noise and interruptions, but also helps foster a mindset congenial to work. In this regard, the physical setting may help act out the appropriate role, as in a theatre, the stage props help actors 'feel' the appropriate role (Ahrentzen, 1990; Gurstein, 1991). Office environments are deliberately designed to limit socializing, eating and other distractions, and at home many people need a distinctive work-only setting.

Temporal boundaries

Teleworkers may find the time demands of work and family life overlap, and they need to be clear about what each role requires and the extent to which it is predictable. Working between 9 and 5 serves these functions in conventional work, and while some workers keep standard working hours, others have good reasons for preferring a different schedule. Managers will find that where contact with colleagues or clients is not a problem, flexibility is generally rewarded with higher productivity and satisfaction. Flexibility is particularly attractive to home-based workers with young children, and to those who find their maximum concentration and creativity outside standard hours (Bailyn,

1989). Increasingly, however, non-standard hours are driven by business needs, for instance where it is not economical to open a large office for computer maintenance functions or where workers interact with people in other time zones. Whether through choice or imposed by the work, the temporal boundary must fit with the daily cycle of household activity and with the workers' physiological needs – long-term disruption of diurnal rhythms may lead to tiredness or poor performance.

Work/family boundaries

Although most writers stress that work and child-minding are incompatible (e.g. Olson, 1989), children or spouses are often present in the home during work (Ahrentzen, 1990). Children can create stress even when the worker is not doing the caring (Olson, 1989), and a suitable boundary requires more than a closed door. Family members must support the arrangement emotionally, and be able to operate independently. The separation of work is not always easily arranged, as instances of conflict, stress and depression show (Salomon and Salomon, 1984; Gurstein, 1991). Although it goes beyond standard management procedures, it may be useful to ask home-based workers about family attitudes to work at home (see Omari and Standen, Chapter 12).

Role conflict may be exacerbated by the different expectations held by women and men. While women are increasing their participation in the workforce, they still carry the greater share of domestic roles (Lewis and Cooper, 1987). Because women have a greater combined load (Pleck, 1985), in telework they may experience greater role conflict, and even more so if men resent them mixing telework with domestic work. There are also different expectations about separation from children. One American study found that women were less likely to have a separate workspace, and that while fathers preferred to be as far away as possible, mothers preferred a separate workspace close to the children (Gurstein, 1991). The women, however, were often unable to find a separate workspace. Another study found that women did more restructuring of work time and space, and reported more family conflict (Rowe and Bentley, 1992). Gender expectations also affect workers' spouses: women who do not work may resent male partners taking over their territory (Salomon and Salmon, 1984), for example.

In the future, research may also help predict role conflict as an outcome of family type. Like individuals and organizations, families vary in their preference for change or stability. One classification contrasts 'closed families', who seek to maintain the status quo; 'open families', who seek a mix of continuity and innovation and allow greater individual action; and 'random families', who revel in variety and change and are highly individualistic (Kantor and Lehr, 1975). It can be imagined that the introduction of a new work role in closed families may be more difficult, whilst for random families too much change and variety may bring conflict with the regular demands of work. Although the attitudes and beliefs of families are not yet well known to either researchers (but see Christensen, 1988) or managers, we need to recognize that some homes are more amenable to telework than others.

Work/community boundaries

Community members often view home-based work as a less serious form of work (e.g. Ahrentzen, 1990). Neighbours, schools and business people assume that home-based work is more interruptible than office work, and home-based workers need to establish a boundary around their work in the minds of community members, usually through a continuing process of education.

The home-based worker's own work/community boundary is also important. Anthropologists and psychologists describe humans as highly territorial animals given to forming attachments with spaces. People personalize and demarcate significant places not only to create privacy but to assert their identity (Altman, 1975). In Western societies the home is particularly important as a buffer from external pressures and a source of one's identity (Ahrentzen, 1990; Guiliani, 1991). Bringing work into this space reduces its value as a sanctuary and source of identity, turning home-based workers into 'officelivers' as one put it (Gurstein, 1991). Those restricted to the home outside work, such as women with domestic responsibilities or people with a disability, may find work at home makes it even more of a prison.

Homework and autonomy

The extent to which people have control over their lives is a major influence on mental health and work performance (Warr, 1987). In telework, control can reduce the impact of role conflict. One study of professional home-based workers found that they experience role overlap but not high levels of conflict (Ahrentzen, 1990), while in another women clerical workers with few employment options, lower work autonomy and greater family demands consistently reported lower well-being (Olson and Primps, 1984).

Compared to office work, telework can increase or decrease autonomy in both work and home-life. The discretion that managers give to teleworkers varies but there is a tendency to increase control, monitoring or formalization out of fear that employees will not perform as well without face-to-face management. Much research shows that work at home is valued by both professional and clerical workers for the increase in discretion it brings (e.g. Christensen, 1988; Leidner, 1988; Bailyn, 1989; Olson, 1989), whether choosing how to do tasks, their order, extent of office attendance or just hours of work. Even control over work breaks, clothing and the layout, decoration, lighting or ventilation of the office can be highly valued.

Managers sensitive to the strong attraction of autonomy will act to enhance it by giving reasonable discretion, avoiding unnecessary monitoring and giving more self-contained tasks (see Daniels, Chapter 8). A strong impression from research is that many home-based workers – professional and clerical – are strongly motivated, highly productive individuals who value home-based work, even when it involves trade-offs (e.g. Olson, 1989). Despite this, some companies demand normal business dress, work hours, and even that employees leave the front door of the house at 9 a.m. and enter the office by a separate door. This is unnecessary and demotivating to many individuals, and those who need such structure will usually create it for themselves. Home-based teleworkers are usually motivated to retain what they see as a privileged option.

Autonomy is also a feature of the worker–family relationship. If home-based work reduces the autonomy of the worker in the family, perhaps through role conflict or time pressure, its success will be limited. There is a gender dimension here too; fathers may use the arrangement to increase leisure time (Olson and Primps, 1984) or may expect family life to fit around work demands (Leidner, 1988). There is less evidence of mothers having more leisure or fewer domestic chores as a result of telework.

Equity in home-based telework

Well-being and performance at home will also be a function of employment conditions. In sending office workers home, some companies have moved them to contract status, reduced wages or benefits, switched to piecework or hourly rates, reduced the amount of work available and even asked staff to pay for equipment (e.g. Leidner, 1988). This may be possible in any form of telework, but workers based entirely or largely at home have the added disadvantage of less visibility to unions, the public or government bodies, and less ability to complain or instigate collective action. The lack of alternative employment for those constrained by family care or disability further increases the risk of poor pay and conditions. Perceived inequity can reduce morale and performance, and while in an office this might be offset by social support from fellow workers, at home the effects will be both less visible and more problematic.

Social value of home-based telework

Home-based work is often perceived in stereotyped ways by managers and employees, more so than other forms of telework. Many managers still see it as an option only for those with a good reason for not attending the office, such as women with young children or people with prolonged illness. Others may have wider criteria but still imagine applicants are not serious about their career, failing to recognize the variety of motivations with positive consequences for organizations (see Omari and Standen, Chapter 12).

Home-based work is also devaluing for a quite different reason: by reducing visibility, and opportunities for networking and self-promotion, it limits career prospects (see Daniels, Chapter 8). While some may accept this as a trade-off for greater life satisfaction or family benefits, all workers should devise strategies to remind the organization of their value, including regular visits to the office or using e-mail or the telephone to maintain support networks. The problem may be exacerbated for women: if they do not have equal status in the organization generally, home-based work can make them even less visible (Leidner, 1988).

Social contact

While reduced contact with other staff is a feature of all telework arrangements, nomadic workers and telecentre workers have contacts with clients or other people that are not available to home-based workers, and social isolation is a major concern. Long-term isolation can affect motivation, work output and psychological well-being. In Chapter 8, Daniels discusses strategies that managers can use to combat isolation. At the same time it is worth considering that home-based workers may have less overall need for socializing, or may get their needs met from non-work sources (Omari and Standen, Chapter 12).

Managing the work/home interface

We have seen that home-based workers must manage not only distance from the organization but also family and community relationships. They need to take more responsibility for their own health, safety and psychological well-being at work. The list of *potential* problems includes family conflict, work interruptions, social isolation, exploitation, corporate invisibility, overwork and lowered status. It is significant, then, that research usually shows satisfaction with home-based work. This is a reflection of the importance of the strategies that workers and managers use to alleviate potential difficulties, including:

- choosing the right type of arrangement, perhaps starting with low contact jobs teleworked one or two days a week;
- selecting individuals who are confident of managing home and community relationships; and whose families are supportive (see Omari and Standen, Chapter 12);
- matching the conditions of telework to employees' circumstances;
- not unnecessarily restricting teleworker autonomy;
- keeping home-based workers 'in the loop' and helping them maintain profile;
- avoiding inequitable employment conditions and benefits;
- making explicit provision for socialization (see Billsberry, Chapter 5);
- advancing the status of home-based work as a valid and valuable work option;
- ensuring that supervisors understand the particular issues faced by teleworkers.

Reports of high satisfaction with home-based telework also reflect the significant personal benefits of telework, including better work/family balance, lower work costs, reduced commuting stress, greater flexibility in work hours, increased autonomy, avoidance of unwanted socialization and better conditions for work, especially where concentration or flexibility are helpful. Studies consistently show that even though satisfaction with the job may be lower (if social contact, work variety or meaningfulness suffer, for example), home-based workers are generally very motivated and productive (e.g. Bailyn, 1989).

Managers should be aware of the role of motivation in explaining this paradox. Teleworkers are often focused on intrinsic aspects of the job such as the work itself or the chance to use or update skills. 'Instrumental' factors, such as career progression and office socialization, may be less important than for traditional workers (see Omari and Standen, Chapter 12). The most common reasons for home-based working are to facilitate childcare for women with children, and to create better working conditions for men and for women without children (Gurstein, 1991). In both cases, telework can be seen as a trade-off: career prospects, job satisfaction and social relationships may be foregone for access to work or better working conditions. These trade-offs can be quite complex, involving factors such as personality, economic circumstances, life goals and stage of working life. They can be expected to become more common in the future as workforce diversity increases, work and career opportunities become less predictable and workers seek greater work/family balance.

Managing home-based teleworkers is made easier by understanding their motivations and the link to productivity and satisfaction, remembering that motivations and home circumstances vary considerably. The research suggests that with appropriate management attitudes and strategies, home-based telework can be a worthwhile option for many more workers than at present.

Notes

[1]This chapter is based on recent Australian research, involving teleworker interviews and manager surveys, which confirm the findings of the published studies mentioned. Further details are available from the author.

References

Ahrentzen, S. (1990) Managing conflict by managing boundaries: How professional homeworkers cope with multiple roles at home. *Environment and Behavior*, **22**, 723–52.

Altman, I. (1975) *The Environment and Social Behavior.* Monterey, CA: Brooks/Cole.

Bailyn, L. (1989) Towards the perfect workplace. *Communications of the Association for Computing Machinery*, **32**, 460–71.

Brief, A.P. (1985) Effects of work location on motivation. In M.H. Olson (ed.) *Office Workstations in the Home.* Washington, DC: National Academy Press.

Christensen, K.E. (1988) *Women and Homebased Work: The Unspoken Contract.* New York: Henry Holt.

Giuliani, M.V. (1991) Towards an analysis of the mental representations of attachment to the home. *The Journal of Architecture and Planning Research*, **8**, 133–46.

Greenhaus, J.H. and Benthell, H.J. (1985) Sources of conflict between work and family roles. *Academy of Management Review*, **10**, 76–88.

Gurstein, P. (1991) Working at home: Emerging scenarios. *Journal of Architecture and Planning Research*, **8**, 164–80.

Hackman, J.R. and Oldham, G. (1980) *Work Redesign.* Reading, MA: Addism-Wesley.

Hartman, R.I., Stoner, C.R. and Arora, R. (1991) An investigation of selected variables affecting telecommuting productivity and satisfaction. *Journal of Business and Psychology,* **6**, 207–25.

Kantor D. and Lehr. W. (1975) *Inside the Family: Toward a Theory of Family Process*. New York: Harper.

Kraut, R.E. (1987) Predicting the use of technology: The case of telework. In R.E. Kraut (ed.) *Technology and the Transformation of White Collar Work*. Hillsdale, NJ: Erlbaum.

Lambert, S.J. (1990) Processes linking work and family; a critical review and research agenda. *Human Relations,* **43**, 239–58.

Leidner, R. (1988) Homework: A study in the interaction of work and family organization. *Research in the Sociology of Work,* **4**, 69–94.

Lewis, S. and Cooper, C.L. (1987) Stress in dual earner couples and stage in life cycle. *Journal of Occupational Psychology,* **60**, 289–303.

Lewis, S. and Cooper, C.L. (1995) Balancing the work/home interface: a European perspective. *Human Resource Management Review,* **5**, 289–305.

Olson, M.H. and Primps, S. (1984) Working at home with computers: Work and non-work issues. *Journal of Social Issues,* **40**, 97–112.

Olson, M.H. (1987) Telework: Practical experience and future prospects. In R.E. Kraut (ed.) *Technology and the Transformation of White Collar Work*. Hillsdale, NJ: Erlbaum.

Olson, M.H. (1989) Work at home for computer professionals: current attitudes and future prospects. *Association for Computing Machinery Transaction on Office Information Systems,* **7**, 317–38.

Pleck, J.H. (1985) *Working Wives/Working Husbands*. Beverley Hills, CA: Sage.

Rowe, B.R. and Bentley, M.T. (1992) The impact of the family on home-based work. *Journal of Family and Economic Issues,* **13**, 279–97.

Salomon, I. and Salomon, M. (1984) Telecommuting: the employee's perspective. *Technological and Social Change,* **25**, 15–28.

Shamir, B. and Salomon, I. (1985) Work-at-home and the quality of working life. *Academy of Management Review,* **10**, 455–64.

Sieber, S.D. (1974) Toward a theory of role accumulation. *American Sociological Review,* **39**, 567–78.

Toffler, A. (1980) *The Third Wave*. New York: William Morrow and Co.

Warr, P. (1987) *Work, Unemployment and Mental Health*. Oxford University Press, Oxford.

Zedeck, S. and Mosier, K.L. (1990) Work in the family and employing organization. *American Psychologist,* **45**, 240–25.

Chapter 10

Teleworking and the psychological contract: a new division of labour?

Paul Sparrow

The psychological contract literature implies a diffuse employment relationship, in which employees each have a set of expectations of what the individual and the organization expect to give and receive in the working relationship (Rousseau, 1990). Contracts are unwritten, open-ended agreements on what is given and what is to be received and are concerned with the social and emotional aspects of the exchange between employer and employee. They are dynamic, with new items added over time and expectations changed as perceptions about the employer's commitment evolve (Robinson *et al.*, 1994; Herriot, 1995). They represent a set of reciprocal expectations. Changes in the contract are assumed to have implications for employee behaviours in response to organizational attempts to manage careers, rewards and commitment. Many distinctions have been drawn between 'old' and 'new' psychological contracts in relation to traditional employment (Ehrlich, 1994; Rousseau, 1995; Sparrow, 1996). The 'old' contract, generated in a period of full employment, stability, growth and predictability, was built on steady financial rewards, investment in training and expectations of advancement, in return for hard work and loyalty. Employees exchanged compliance for security (Spindler, 1994). The new contract is seen as being based on the concept of 'employability' in which people: cannot expect guarantees of employment security and may in fact feel lucky to have a job; should expect promotion to be reserved for those who deserve it and for performance to be rewarded; can expect higher levels of responsibility but also accountability; earn status not through time served but on the basis of competence and credibility; take personal responsibility for their own development; and place their trust in their profession or project, but less so their organization.

Cascio (1998) notes that in the USA, largely as a function of a vibrant expanding economy, many employers are rethinking how to help their valued workers strike a better balance between their work and personal lives whilst also serving customers better. Teleworking is one outcome from this re-evaluation of how work is performed, managed and rewarded. Indeed, by changing the way that work is done, it is argued that a new kind of economy is emerging centred on the individual, in which tasks are no longer assigned and controlled through a stable chain of management, but are carried out autonomously by independent contractors (Malone and Laubacher, 1998). The move away from an employment relationship in the context of large organizations – and its reflection in the psychological contract – is evident. Twenty-five years ago, one in five US workers were employed by a Fortune 500 company, whereas today it is one in ten. Indeed the largest private employer in the USA is not General Motors or IBM; it is the temporary employment agency Manpower Inc., which had 2 million people on its books in 1997.

Rhetoric says that teleworking affords employers the opportunity to improve employee motivation and develop management styles based on trust, open communications and self-management. However, an economy based more on small and temporary organizations reliant on virtual working methods still carries risks (Malone and Laubacher, 1998, p. 152):

> … an e-lance economy might lead to disruption and dislocation. Loosed from its traditional moorings, the business world might become chaotic and cutthroat. The gap between society's haves and have-nots might widen, as those lacking special talents or access to electronic networks fall by the wayside.

This chapter argues that the psychological reactions to, and accommodation of, teleworking will be complex and subject to wide individual differences. Using the concept of the psychological contract helps provide some insights into just what some of the management issues will be.

The content of the psychological contract

Herriot *et al.* (1997) examined the perceived mutual obligations of 184 UK managers and 184 UK employees across a range of sectors and found that 18 constructs captured the perception of mutual obligations. Organizations had seven categories of obligation expected of employees: to work contracted hours; to do a quality piece of work; to deal honestly with clients; to be loyal and guard the organization's reputation; to treat property carefully; to dress and behave correctly; and to be flexible and go beyond one's job description. It is input, not output, that matters to the employer.

What does the employee expect of the employer? Eleven constructs were revealed: to provide adequate induction and training; to ensure fairness in selection, appraisal, promotion and redundancy procedures; to provide justice, fairness and consistency in the application of rules and disciplinary procedures; to provide equitable pay in relation to market values across the organization; to be fair in the allocation of benefits; to allow time off to meet family and personal needs; to consult and communicate on matters that affect them; to interfere minimally with employees in terms of *how* they do their job; to act in a personally supportive way to employees; to recognize or reward special contribution or long service; to provide a safe and congenial work environment; and to provide what job security they can. This understanding about the basic territory of the contract makes it easier for both parties to establish a 'fair exchange deal'.

One way of understanding what is important to employees employed on a teleworking basis is to examine the collective agreements negotiated by unions on their behalf. Reflecting the basic contractual elements identified by Herriot *et al.* (1997), some unions in the UK are seeking agreements that teleworking should always be voluntary, employees should have the right to return to office-based working, there should be clarity about whether the individual remains an employee with full rights or becomes a self-employed contractor, rates of pay and benefits, annual leave, pensions and perks such as childcare provision should be the same, and the contract of employment should require regular opportunities to meet with staff and colleagues to avoid isolation (*Management Today*, 1998). One of the first flexible working agreements struck in the UK was the Co-operative Bank's teleworking agreement (Flexible Working, 1997). The agreement struck between the bank and the Banking Insurance and Finance Union laid down a framework for remote working that included provision of equipment, special allowances, insurance and training. The bank wanted an agreement about tele-working as part of a general deal about flexible working and job-sharing. The union's main concern was that staff should not feel cut off from their colleagues and should be no worse off financially for working at home. Regular meetings and communication with line managers is specified in the agreement.

Another way is to consider the main motives for teleworking. This indicates some areas of 'the deal' that will be important should they not be delivered. The study by Baruch and Nicholson (1997), for example, found that the main motives of teleworkers were: the reduced need for travel; improved quality of work life; and the higher quality and volume of work that become possible. Flexible working hours, flexible methods of work and easier childcare arrange-ments were only secondary considerations.

Will all teleworkers have the same type of psychological contract? Certainly not. Rousseau (1995) identified four types of contract, dependent on whether: the performance terms were specified or unspecified; and whether the duration of the relationship was short term or long term. As with traditional employment, all four types of psychological contract can be expected to exist across the different variants of telework. Taking each quadrant and applying it to the telework envi-ronment, we should expect to see the types of contract shown in Table 10.1.

Given this variety of possible contract types within a teleworking envi-ronment, we should expect to see people fight to move into the more long-term duration and 'insider' type of telework. There will be a new division of labour based around the type of contract offered by the telework variant.

Formation of psychological contracts

In Chapter 5, Billsberry looks at the issue of socialization primarily in terms of values-fit. If this exists between the employee and organization then it can serve as a control mechanism (as a substitute for a strong psychological contract, one might speculate). The selection process is stressed as a mechanism

TABLE 10.1 Different types of psychological contracts for teleworkers

Type	Context	Characteristics	Examples
Transactional	Limited duration and well specified in performance terms	Low ambiguity, easy exit and high turnover, low member commitment, freedom to enter new contracts, little learning, weak integration/identification	Short telework tasks done in a decentralized environment such as data entry, computer code writing, editing, typing
Transitional	'No guarantees' type of condition where there has been a breakdown of psychological contracts, reflecting an absence of commitment regarding future employment (short term) but with little or no explicit performance demands	Ambiguity, uncertainty, high turnover, high termination, and instability	Telework arrangements foisted on employees as part of a cost-cutting process, or researchers and hired hands who work on subcontracted but open-ended information searches, speech briefs, synopses for others to add value to
Relational	Open-ended, longer-term or relationship-orientated employment, but with incomplete or ambiguous performance requirements attached to continued membership of the network	High member commitment, high affective commitment, high integration/identification, and stability	Trusted problem solving 'hit' teams brought in to turn a project around, networked consultancies drawing upon specific experts when required, educational and publication consortiums mobilizing trainers and writers for specific projects, small production sub-units or teams that work together selling their craft within a larger network of people
Balanced	Open-ended, relationship-orientated, high involvement work but with well-specified performance terms that might be subject to change over time	High member commitment, high integration/identification, ongoing development, mutual support, dynamic	Virtual teamworking, telework occupations where individuals identify more with their craft (such as the creative elements of film production, video-editing), and consultants in a preferred partnership type of arrangement.

for doing this. However, in many cases, especially teleworking-to-teleworking collaborations in short-term projects, participants will be selected primarily for their technical skill and knowledge domain. The luxury of selecting on values might not always be a viable option.

There is then, a deeper challenge – if I cannot always select people to match my values, can I socialize them into an appropriate and matched psychological contract? In her socio-cognitive theory of contract formation, Rousseau (1995) argues that contracts are mental models in which people interpret the promises they perceive have been made. Differences in each person's model reflect the different information available to the interpreter. She has shown that contracts are formed through interactions (with people such as recruiters, managers, co-workers and mentors) and through the social cues picked up through observation. For some teleworkers, much of this interaction and observation will be perceived only through the lens of electronic media. There are two major issues:

1. The number of 'agents' from whom cues will be picked up multiplies in a decentralized or networked environment. This means that the behaviour of agents cannot be controlled by the principal contract maker, and also that the individual finds it much harder to attribute blame or perceived breach of contract.
2. The socialization processes through which the contract is formed could take on a very different form.

The biggest problem here is that organizations could lose control over the 'decoding process' (Rousseau, 1995). Decoding refers to the judgements that people make regarding the standards of behaviour that must be met in order to fulfil commitments made by themselves or the organization – for example, does loyalty mean saying nice things about people outside work, or is criticizing the organization to make it more effective an acceptable form of behaviour? The ability to create such normative contracts will be diminished when the same interpretation of events cannot be established across the network of teleworkers. This augers towards a more individualized and low-trust environment in what is supposed to be a high-trust/high-dependency work form. Given this, pressure will be placed on networked organizations to find alternative ways of creating a strong culture. Establishing a culture from scratch, or selecting to it on the basis of values, might be a solution for small start-up electronic ventures, or craft-based teleworkers (such as graphic designers or film makers) who already have their own strong occupational cultures.

Will these issues be any different in an extremely team-focused virtual environment? Virtual teams are far more likely to involve far more diverse and transient membership across different geographical locations within the organization; contingent workers from outside the organization; suppliers and customers; and even resource providers from many different cultures. They should be expected to operate within multiple (and even competing) alliances both within and outside the virtual team. Although all parties are interdependent, as an individual it might be far more difficult to reduce life to simple certainties such as 'who is "us"', 'who are "they"', and 'who is "me"'?

With whom am I making an implicit deal? Who or what therefore might breach this deal? This increased diversity of interdependence might be interpreted in one of two ways: the potential for breach of contract will be multiplied; or the psychological contract will be so diffuse and weak that it will be an irrelevance in a teleworking setting.

The transactional nature of the psychological contract may well be reinforced by the attitude that organizations take to teleworkers in terms of the level of incentive, shared risk and reward offered. The trade-off between incentives and control seems to lie at the heart of how effective the relationship is. Analysing the relationship between innovation and virtual organization, Chesbrough and Teece (1996) identified situations where the virtual relationship can become counter-productive. For example, in Sun Microsystems, much has been made of the way in which businesses and individuals are coordinated as free agents who come together to buy and sell one another's goods and services. But outside developers of workstation software could obtain greater rewards by selling software to Sun customers than by developing the same software as a Sun employee, if they were prepared to move faster, work harder and take more risks. High-powered market-based incentives such as stock options and attractive bonuses made it easy for small virtual organizations to gain access to the people they needed. However, as personal rewards became larger and more was at stake, each party to joint development acted in their own self-interest, and irresolvable conflicts arose. Tacit knowledge and information, often vital to an innovation, also tends to diffuse more slowly over virtual networks (cf. Tregaskis and Daniels, Chapter 13).

Contract violations

Contract violations start with a perceived discrepancy in outcome. The problem with contract violation is that some events seemingly at odds with an individual's interests might not provoke an adverse reaction whilst another innocuous event can engender outrage and anger. By applying Rousseau's (1995) model of contract violation to the teleworking environment, we can predict new instances of violation. Loss of reputation in a remote and networked environment where your next contract depends on its maintenance could be an important driver. Teleworkers whose livelihood depends on reputation will soon learn to manage their own reputation more jealously and to monitor it in others. Delivering on time in a mutually dependent environment will sadly become more important than the quality of thinking behind the delivery in the short term. There are three sources of reputational breach that matter in traditional employment (Rousseau, 1995) and that will matter for teleworkers: failure to cooperate; opportunism; and negligence.

- *Failure to cooperate:* Norms regarding good faith and fair dealing are there to be breached in a teleworking environment. What things will tempt a teleworker to stop cooperating and mistrust someone in the system? The new triggers for breach will likely include access rights to information, ownership of 'gatekeeper' roles, rights to be able to modify information, intellectual property rights and perceived plagiarism.

- *Opportunism:* Active self-serving behaviour by one party at the expense of another is another major source of breach. Teleworkers will easily breach others' contracts by: quitting specific tasks at short notice or letting these tasks 'drop' from their priorities without informing others (easy to do when not supervised); using the power ceded to them as brokers of information to renegotiate their own terms and conditions; and being seen to or found out copying or forwarding e-mail to different parties with different interpretations of events.
- *Negligence:* Passive breach of contract, where there is a failure to perform specified responsibilities. Such negligence will be easy in a telework environment where there is often: more autonomy; a lack of control within the network of information flows; more dependence on other people and trust that they will 'handle their bit of the piece' professionally; more opportunity for information overload and the consequential dysfunctional decision making.

Conclusions

It is possible to foresee a scenario where what is a high-trust work form – teleworking – will lead to so many breaches of psychological contract that it will actually become a distrustful form of work. Breach of psychological contract in telework environments will become an important research topic. Trust is surely as important an issue with teleworking as it has proved to be for the psychological contract amongst 'old deal' employees.

But what will be the new bases of trust between teleworkers and the providers of their work (not necessarily their employer), and the new opportunities for breach of trust? In a teleworking environment primary interactions take place through electronic media. There is understandable concern whether the system is there to monitor and evaluate the individual. The free flow of communication that used to take place in the office environment is unlikely to be replicated by electronic media, as individuals become concerned about privacy and system security (Townsend *et al.*, 1998). Although forward-thinking organizations might establish policies regarding communication privacy in order to convince participants that it is safe to share ideas and concerns across virtual team systems, will they be believed?

Another important dimension to contract violation to be studied will concern the psychological contracts *within and across the household of the teleworker*. The partial dissolution of the boundary between work and non-work changes many relationships (Baruch and Nicholson, 1997) and flexible family life with partners who can adjust the balance of their home/work involvement is important.

This chapter leads to the following conclusions:

- We should not expect that teleworking will prove a panacea for the ills of the existing poor state of the psychological contract in many areas of employment.

- In terms of the territory covered by teleworkers' psychological contracts, many of the basic contractual exchanges seen in traditional employment are just as relevant to teleworkers and can be expected to form the basis of management–union negotiations when employees are transferring to this form of employment.
- We might expect a new division of labour based on the different types of psychological contract that the various forms of telework entail.
- Formation of psychological contracts as a way of regulating employee behaviour will be a much harder process to manage, and the presence of multiple agents in the contract will raise the likelihood of the contract being breached.
- The socialization process will be altered fundamentally as teleworkers view and interpret behaviour through the lens of electronic media.
- Teleworking will generate new examples of breach of contract, especially concerning the issue of reputation.
- It is possible to foresee a scenario in which teleworking rapidly becomes a low-trust work form, despite brave intentions to the contrary.
- We are likely to extend our enquiry to the psychological contracts of all those in the household, not just the teleworker, and will begin to examine the individual work/home life balance behaviour that can avoid this becoming an issue.

References

Baruch, Y. and Nicholson, N. (1997) Home, sweet work: requirements for effective home working. *Journal of General Management*, **23**, 15–30.

Cascio, W.F. (1998) On managing a virtual workplace. *The Occupational Psychologist*, **35**, 5–11.

Chesbrough, H.W. and Teece, D.J. (1996) When is virtual virtuous? Organizing for innovation. *Harvard Business Review*, **74**, 65–73.

Ehrlich, J.C. (1994) Creating an employer–employee relationship for the future. *Human Resource Management*, **33**, 491–501.

Flexible Working (1997) Co-operative Bank's teleworking agreement. *Flexible Working*, **2**, 7 and 18.

Herriot, P. (1995) Psychological contracts. In N. Nicholson (ed.) *Encyclopaedic Dictionary of Organizational Behaviour*. Oxford: Blackwell.

Herriot, P., Manning, W.E.G. and Kidd, J.M. (1997) The content of the psychological contract. *British Journal of Management*, **8**, 151–62.

Malone, T.W. and Laubacher, R.J. (1998) The dawn of the e-lance economy. *Harvard Business Review*, **76**, 145–52.

Management Today (1998) The changing perception of teleworking – time for teleworking. *HR Strategies Update*, April. London: Haymarket Publications.

Robinson, S.L., Kraatz, S.M. and Rousseau, D.M. (1994) Changing obligations and the psychological contract: a longitudinal study. *Academy of Management Journal*, **37**, 137–151.

Rousseau, D.M. (1990) New hire perceptions of their own and their employer's obligations: a study of psychological contracts. *Journal of Organizational Behaviour*, **11**, 389–400.

Rousseau, D.M. (1995) *Psychological Contracts in Organizations: Understanding Written and Unwritten Agreements.* London: Sage.

Sparrow, P.R. (1996) Transitions in the psychological contract in U.K. banking. *Human Resource Management Journal*, **6**, 75–92.

Spindler, S.G. (1994) Psychological contracts in the workplace – a lawyer's view. *Human Resource Management*, **33**, 325–34.

Townsend, A.M., DeMarie, S. and Hendrickson, A.R. (1998) Virtual teams: technology and the workplace of the future. *Academy of Management Executive*, **12**, August, 17–29.

Chapter 11

Managerial style and telework

David Lamond

In Chapter 7, we referred to a University of Michigan report on teleworking (Bolletino *et al.*, 1997), which contained a series of recommendations concerning the personal qualities that should be possessed by teleworkers. The same report also contained a set of recommendations in regard to the qualities that should be possessed by the managers or supervisors of those teleworkers:

> An individual supervising a telework arrangement should ideally have better than average supervisory and communication skills and should be able to clearly define specific tasks and expectations. While true for all jobs, it is especially important for supervisors of employees who are teleworking to review work performance against pre-established objectives.

The report went on to say that supervisors who needed physically to observe their employees working would have to re-orient their management style if they were to contribute properly to the success of telework projects. In this regard, the report talked about the necessity of supervisors trusting their employees. The report expressed the view that those who supervise by 'coaching' rather than 'policing' their staffs would be more suitable for supervising 'off-site' employees. This section of the report concluded with the observation that just as employees must be achievement oriented, supervisors must be results oriented, and that supervisors need to be as supportive of the telework concept as their employees are.

The purpose of this chapter is to examine managerial style in relation to teleworkers and determine the extent to which, as the University of Michigan report suggests, managing teleworkers requires a different approach to managing other workers. We have already hinted in Chapter 3 that there is a temptation, in this 'brave new world' of teleworking and virtual organizations, to get carried away with notions of virtuality, and to label virtually everything associated with these changed work and organizational forms as 'new' and 'different'. Often, these labels are used without a reference point – new and different to what? We will therefore begin by establishing a framework of management functions and roles within which we can examine what managers need to do. We can then move on to consider how and why this (what managers do) might be different for workers whom they may not see regularly or may never even meet.

Management and management styles

It might seem quite odd to begin this discussion by proffering a definition of management, since we all know what it is. The problem, however, is that there is very little agreement on what *it* is (Thomas, 1993). A detailed discussion of *it* is beyond the scope of this chapter (see e.g. Lamond, 1996, 1998a, 1998b), but it is important to outline briefly the model of management which informs the discussion here. It is a twofold model, built on the twin pillars of the functions of management outlined by Fayol (1949) and the roles managers enact as they carry out those functions, as elaborated by Mintzberg (1973).

Fayol (1949) defines management in terms of the well-known five functions – planning, organizing, commanding (leading, in modern parlance), coordinating and controlling. As Fayol (1949, pp. 5–6) says, to manage is '… to forecast and plan, to organize, to command, to co-ordinate and to control'. Planning means 'examining the future and drawing up the plan of action'. Organizing means 'building up the dual structure, material and human, of the undertaking'. Commanding means 'maintaining activity among the personnel'. Coordinating means 'binding together, unifying and harmonizing all activity and effort'. Controlling means 'seeing that everything occurs in conformity with established rule and expressed command'.

While Fayol's characterization has been subject to a range of criticisms over the years, it still represents the most useful way to conceptualize a manager's job (Carroll and Gillen 1987; Thomas, 1993; Lamond, 1998b). When we think about these functions in relation to teleworkers, we know that managers still need to plan their work; ensure that the necessary resources (financial, material and human) are available to them; lead and motivate them; harmonize their activities; and evaluate the outcomes of their efforts and modify their activities accordingly.

What do managers *do* as they carry out these functions? Mintzberg (1973) identifies a series of interpersonal, informational and decisional roles that managers enact, which are summarized in Table 11.1. Again, when we consider Mintzberg's (1973) manager roles in relation to teleworkers and teleworking, they will still need to carry out ceremonial activities (welcomes, farewells); carry out managerial activities involving subordinates; engage in activities involving outsiders; handle the mail and other contacts concerned primarily with receiving information; forward mail to the organization for informational purposes, and have contacts involving information flow to subordinates; inform key influencers and the organization's public; engage in strategy and review sessions involving initiation or design of improvement projects and/or disturbances and crises; activities involving budgeting and the programming of subordinates' work; and contract and labour negotiations.

Reviewing both these approaches to understanding management reminds us that it is not the manager's roles and responsibilities that will change as we

TABLE 11.1   The manager's working roles (adapted from Mintzberg, 1973, pp. 92–3)

Role	Description	Examples of activities
Interpersonal		
Figurehead	Symbolic head; obliged to perform a number of routine duties of a legal or social nature	Ceremony; status requests; solicitations
Leader	Motivation and activation of subordinates; responsible for staffing, training and associated duties	Virtually all managerial activities involving subordinates
Liaison	Maintains self-developed network of outside contacts and informers who provide favours and information	Acknowledgment of mail; external board work; other activities involving outsiders
Informational		
Monitor	Seeks and receives wide variety of special information (much of it current) to develop thorough understanding of organization and environment; emerges as nerve centre of internal and external information of the organization	Handling all mail and contacts categorized as concerned primarily with receiving information (e.g. periodical news, observational tours)
Disseminator	Transmits information received from outsiders or from other subordinates to members of the organization; some information factual, some involving interpretation and integration of diverse value positions of organizational influencers	Forwarding mail to organization for informational purposes, verbal contacts involving information flow to subordinates (e.g. review sessions, instant communication flows)
Spokesperson	Dissemination of the organization's information to its environment	Inform 'key influencers' (e.g. CEO, Board) and 'the organization's public' (suppliers, trade organizations, peers, government agencies, customers and press)
Decisional		
Entrepreneur	Searches organization and its environment for opportunities and initiates 'improvement projects' to bring about change; supervises design of certain projects as well	Strategy and review sessions involving initiation or design of improvement projects
Disturbance handler	Responsible for corrective action when organization faces important, unexpected disturbances	Strategy and review sessions involving disturbances and crises
Resource allocator	Responsible for the allocation of organizational resources of all kinds –in effect the making or approval of all significant organizational decisions	Scheduling; requests for authorization; any activity involving budgeting and the programming of subordinates' work
Negotiator	Responsible for representing the organization at major negotiations	Contract negotiation, labour negotiations

move from traditional work forms to teleworking. Rather, it is the way these roles and responsibilities are enacted that may change. Think, for example, of how the role of Hamlet has been enacted, first several decades ago by English actor Sir Laurence Olivier and then, more recently, by Australian Mel Gibson – they both enacted the same role (indeed, they were even required to say the same words), but proffered very different interpretations in *how* they enacted the role. Modern-day managers may now engage in *participative* decision making to make provision for the future, and coordinate their subordinates in *teams* rather than as individuals, but they still have to plan and coordinate. In the same way, the managers of teleworkers still have to carry out their managerial functions, albeit perhaps, in different ways.

With this in mind, we will now explore the management of teleworkers. First, we should note that teleworking is, of itself, a management 'style'. By this we mean that teleworking is one of a number of flexible working practices (e.g. part-time, temporary or casual employment; overtime and shift working; contracting) which have grown in recent times as a way of making sure that the necessary human resources are matched to the work of the organization (e.g. Brewster *et al.*, 1994). The introduction of this style of managing workers may be driven by, for example, business needs to increase organizational efficiency and productivity, or by an effort to provide to employees an opportunity to balance work and family needs (see Standen, Chapter 4). Either way, teleworking represents a particular approach to, for example, planning and coordinating the work to be done and providing the necessary resources to ensure the work to be done *is* done. Whether this is a new and fundamentally different approach to what has gone before is, however, open to question. This question is examined in the next section.

Managing teleworkers: the need for a 'new' style

A detailed account of *all* the ways in which teleworking, as a form of work, influences the way that teleworkers should be managed is beyond the scope of this chapter. At the same time, as Evans (1994) has found with her study of home-workers, for example, it is the 'people management' issues, and the matter of supervision in particular, that were the main concern of the managers who were going to be supervising the homeworkers. The most useful focus here, then, is on those aspects of management that relate to the question 'How do you manage the performance of people that you may never see?' We will now consider each of the features of teleworking as we have defined it – location, ICTs, knowledge intensity, intra-organizational contact and extra-organizational contact – and how these may influence the way we go about carrying out this set of managerial tasks.

Location

By definition, teleworkers spend at least a proportion, if not all, of their working time away from the central office. This distance between the teleworkers, their managers/supervisors and each other creates a number of problems to which their managers need to be alert and develop appropriate strategies to overcome

(Metzger and Von Glinow, 1988). For example, as teleworkers have less involvement with the organization and with co-workers, so traditional rewards, with the exception of money and cash-measured benefits, are available less (it is difficult to pat someone on the back over the Internet). On the other hand, it is likely that many of those workers, particularly those with qualifications and engaging in high intensity knowledge work, will respond better to the non-cash incentives and rewards (Metzger and Von Glinow, 1988). Managers will therefore need to be alert to the reward systems they implement and look for creative, non-cash, ways of motivating, recognizing and rewarding desired behaviour. For example, providing additional training (for those individuals who place a high value on mastery of knowledge and skills), or job enrichment (where more challenging tasks are built into the job responsibilities) are ways in which the efforts of knowledge workers can be recognized and rewarded.

One way of doing this is to look for ways to increase the interaction with and between the teleworkers. Communication is the social glue that ties members, teams and organizations together (Rapert and Wren, 1998). Teleworkers can overcome the geographic and time dispersion they may experience, to the extent that their information and communication technologies provide them with access to an enriched communication medium, and managers are responsible for providing that medium.

At the same time, Gordon and Kelly (1986, p. 75) stress the difference between *close* supervision and *good* supervision. Managers who have frequent, close contact with their subordinates in the office can develop the habit of letting that contact take the place of more disciplined approaches to supervision. More formal assessment of progress, where regularly scheduled meetings to discuss key events or milestones are held, can be replaced by the question 'How's the project going?' and the reply of 'Just fine, thanks' as managers and their subordinates pass in the corridor. This may be a habit to be overcome and replaced as location reduces the opportunities for that kind of interaction (assuming it is appropriate in the first place).

Invisibility is another problem of location. Career progression is, in part at least, a function of *visible* performance and success. This visibility is often absent for teleworkers (Metzger and Von Glinow, 1988). It is likely that this is also the case when candidates for training and development programmes are being considered. One way of overcoming this problem is through 'spotlighting' (Gordon and Kelly, 1986, pp. 81–2) – taking advantage of or creating opportunities for the exposure of the performance of teleworkers for the benefit of senior management. For example, managers can use the periodic visits to the office to organize group presentations or participation in important project groups, or simply a lunch meeting with the boss.

Information and communication technologies (ICTs)

The leaps in development of information and communication technologies (ICTs) over the past decade can be seen as both blessing and curse when it comes to the management of teleworkers. On the one hand, because information can be shared instantly and inexpensively among many people in many locations, it is possible for individuals to manage themselves and coordinate their efforts through their electronic links (Malone and Laubacher, 1998). Townsend *et al.* (1998) are confident that, while the dispersal of teleworkers means that effective supervision and control may appear problematic, the richness of the communicative environment (provided by way of ICTs) may mean that there is a capacity for more managerial monitoring rather than less in regard to the traditional environment; for example, the manager can review archived recordings of team meetings to assess member contribution and team progress. That is not to say that monitoring, *per se*, is the same as effective supervision. Rather, Townsend *et al.*'s (1998) observation signals to us that we do have access to the kinds of data that can be used as a basis for negotiating and agreeing with employees how their performance is to be managed.

On the other hand, one of the problems of ICTs is that they cannot capture the same richness and detail of information as face-to-face communication and being in the same workspace as others (Jackson, 1997). Further, the information from ICTs can be too rich, leading to information overload (see Daniels, Chapter 8). Either way, the teleworker may finish with incomplete information or too much information to screen and assimilate properly. The manager needs to monitor the interactions closely with a view to ensuring that teleworkers get not too much or too little, but sufficient information and interaction. At the same time, the process of managerial monitoring described by Townsend *et al.* (1998) can all too easily become invasive if there isn't a degree of self-monitoring on the part of the manager. It is important that the manager use the available tools to manage and not merely control.

Knowledge intensity

Metzger and Von Glinow (1988) describe what they call the 'control system paradox' in relation to the management of knowledge-based teleworkers. Typically, the more that employees have a valued set of professional skills, the more independent and resistant to controls they become. There is a need, then, to move from managing according to a set of 'means' controls to identifying an appropriate set of 'ends' controls. It is the case for teleworkers, as it is for any group, that managers need to establish clearly expectations about performance and criteria for assessing success. In the case of high knowledge intensity teleworkers, these criteria will be established in terms of schedules for reports, interim deliverables and the final product or service and then measured against them (Townsend *et al.*, 1998).

Low knowledge intensity jobs (particular forms of clerical work, data input and so on) need no less attention in this regard. It is important that the supervision of this group does not become akin to operating a virtual 'process line', where the teleworkers become extensions of the machines into which they are inputting data. As we noted above, there is a difference between close supervision and effective supervision. Similarly, there is a difference between accurate monitoring and interpersonal supervision.

Intra-organizational communication

People with low levels of intra-organizational communication may begin to feel isolated and not part of the organization and managers need to be sensitive to the extent to which this low level of communication exists. Townsend *et al.* (1998) suggest that one approach here, especially where the teleworkers are operating as teams, is to develop their own style of language and communications protocols, no matter how informal, as a way of aiding group cohesion. Over time, the team will develop a variety of methods to ensure that their communication is both efficient and accurate. This might be effective for the individuals and groups who have both the desire and skills to be more self-managing, but in other situations it may be necessary for managers to be more proactive.

In being so, managers might consider initiating a variety of interactions, formal or informal, individual or group based, regularly or irregularly scheduled. Among the strategies here could be the organizing of social activities such as luncheons or office parties; face-to-face information and planning sessions (notwithstanding the availability of groupware); or the establishment of problem-solving groups (quality circles).

Extra-organizational communication

High levels of extra-organizational communication, especially when it is combined with low levels of intra-organizational communication, can add to the sense of isolation (even alienation) from the organization. Managers need to be equally alert to this problem and examine ways they can put themselves into the 'loop', and help workers remain in the loop, in a supportive rather than directive role.

Whitener *et al.* (1998) have discussed the critical role of managers as initiators of trust. This is no different for telework. In each of the aspects of telework, trust has been an implicit denominator of the managerial style discussed – if there is no trust, telework is unlikely to be instituted as a form of work at all. A level of trust is necessary to manage people at a distance; to provide them with the necessary ICTs to carry out their jobs without 'snooping' to ensure they are complying with usage protocols; to deal with high intensity knowledge workers who want to work autonomously and to micro-manage themselves; and to be satisfied that the levels of intra- and extra-organizational communication in which teleworkers engage are necessary and appropriate.

Old wine in new bottles?

In our framework, it is equally important to select the right management style as it is to manage other aspects of telework. What is the 'best' management style? We know from Froggatt (1998) that, at NCR where approximately 20 per cent of its 12,500 strong US workforce is involved in a mandatory teleworking programme, the company has realized a 15–20 per cent productivity improvement since implementing this new way of working. Similarly, Froggatt (1998) reports that Nortel, which has also implemented a teleworking programme for some 2500 of its North American staff, but on a voluntary basis, is meeting its twin goals of improving employee satisfaction and increasing their productivity. Surveys of Nortel staff have found that 80 per cent of teleworkers reported increased satisfaction; 88 per cent reported increased productivity; and individual productivity improved by an average 10–22 per cent (see also Lamond, Chapter 3 for more details).

One message from these results is that there is no 'one best way' to manage teleworkers – one programme is mandatory and the other voluntary, yet both programmes are very successful. Rather this suggests that we need to recognize the importance of adopting an approach, as individual managers and as management collectively, which is consistent with the organization's goals and culture. It is important that managers endeavour to manage by objectives and to provide supportive environments. It is equally important that managers build congruence between organizational cultures and telework practices.

Nearly 15 years ago, Zureik (1985), with some concern, described the experience of teleworkers at the time as in danger of developing into a case of 'old wine in new bottles'. By this, she was referring to the way in which this new form of working was simply reproducing the same gender inequalities as the traditional workplace, where women are slotted into low status jobs and men into higher ones (there is certainly more recent evidence to sustain her proposition; e.g. Crossan and Burton, 1993; Hamblin, 1995). Be that as it may, Zureik (1985) reminds us that much of what is good management of workers in traditional settings is also good management in telework settings, and vice versa – if we are indeed putting old wine in new bottles, let us make sure that we choose the best vintages.

References

Bolletino, L., de Pietro, L., Kari Gluski, K., Lauerman, E., Leacock, G., Lebowitz, L., Martin, N., Ostron, D., Rojo, L. and Steiner, C. (1997) ITD Telecommuting Task Force Report. University of Michigan: http: //www.itd.umich.edu/telecommuting/report/index.html.

Brewster, C., Hegewisch, A. and Mayne, L. (1994) Flexible working practices: the controversy and the evidence. In C. Brewster and A. Hegewisch (eds) *Policy and Practice in European Human Resource Management*. London: Routledge, 168–93.

Carroll, S.J. and Gillen, D.J. (1987) Are the classical management functions useful in describing managerial work? *Academy of Management Review*, **12**, 38–51.

Crossan, G. and Burton, P.F. (1993) Teleworking stereotypes: A case study. *Journal of Information Science Principles & Practice*, **19**, 349–62.

Evans, A. (1994) Working from home: a new career dimension, *International Journal of Career Management*, **5**, 16–25.

Fayol, H. (1949) *General and Industrial Management*. (trans. C Storrs). London: Pitman.

Froggatt, C.C. (1998) Telework: whose choice is it anyway? *Facilities Design & Management*; Spring, 18–21.

Gordon, G.E. and Kelly, M.M. (1986) *Telecommuting: How to Make It Work for You and Your Company.* Englewood Cliffs, NJ: Prentice-Hall.

Hamblin, H. (1995) Employees' perspectives on one dimension of labour flexibility: working at a distance. *Work, Employment and Society, 9*, 473–98.

Jackson, P.J. (1997) Flexibility and rigidity in new forms of work: individual versus organizational issues. Presented at the Congress of the European Association of Work and Organizational Psychologists, Verona, Italy, April.

Lamond, D.A. (1998a) If management is 'common sense', why is sense in management so uncommon? *Journal of the Australian and New Zealand Academy of Management, 4*, 1–9.

Lamond, D.A. (1998b) Back to the future: lessons from the past for a new management era. In G. Griffin (ed.) *Management Theory and Practice: Moving to a New Era.* Melbourne: Macmillan.

Lamond, D.A. (1996) Karpin on management: is that all managers should be doing? *Journal of the Australian and New Zealand Academy of Management, 2*, 21–35.

Malone, T.W. and Laubacher, R.J. (1998) The dawn of the e-lance economy. *Harvard Business Review, 76*, 144–52.

Metzger, R.O. and Von Glinow, M.A. (1988) Off-site workers: At home and abroad. *California Management Review*, Spring, 101–11.

Mintzberg, H. (1973) *The Nature of Managerial Work.* New York: Harper & Row.

Rapert, M.I. and Wren, B.M. (1998) Reconsidering organizational structure: A dual perspective of frameworks and processes. *Journal of Managerial Issues, 10*, 287–302.

Thomas, A.B. (1993) *Controversies in Management.* London: Routledge.

Townsend, A.M., DeMarie, S. and Hendrickson, A.R. (1998) Virtual teams: technology and the workplace of the future. *Academy of Management Executive, 12*, August, 17–29.

Whitener, E.M., Brodt, S.E., Korsgaard, M.A. and Werner, J.M. (1998) Managers as initiators of trust: An exchange relationship framework for understanding managerial trustworthy behaviour. *Academy of Management Review, 23*, 513–30.

Zureik, E.T. (1985) The electronic cottage: old wine in new bottles. Presented at the Conference on Technology and Culture: Computers, Values, Creativity. University of Ottawa, Canada, 8–10 May.

Chapter 12

Selection for telework

Maryam Omari and Peter Standen

Uncertainty about who is suited to telework is a common reason why managers do not make effective use of it. Part of the answer is fairly obvious and has been well documented in numerous practical guides. For example, Kinsman (1987) finds that a teleworker must be self-disciplined, well organized, committed to the job, a good communicator and able to work independently. Research on telework also shows how personality, motivation and skills can predict success in telework, as we discuss later. However, in telework it is also important to look beyond the attributes of the individual. Good performance requires that tasks retain continuity with the organization's technical systems, that the worker maintains good social relations with the organization and its clients, and that the remote environment is conducive to work. Thus, a broad view of selection is required (Figure 12.1). While this may seem complicated, there are many other examples of where new technology will not realize potential gains in flexibility and productivity without significant rethinking of management processes. A useful way to reduce the complexity of such cases is to adopt a systemic approach.

A systemic approach to selection

In an increasingly complex and dynamic business world it becomes harder to identify *the* right way of managing many organizational functions. Rather than follow fixed procedures, managers need to identify underlying forces, and in particular to see how business performance depends on an interconnected set of systems (Senge, 1990). In this context Figure 12.1 is not a prescription but a reminder of key variables that are *potentially* relevant to any good selection process. In our research we find that some firms use telework as an effective and innovative tool, while others use it as a band-aid to cover short-term needs (see Standen, Chapter 4). This difference is reflected in their approaches to selection: one group focuses on how remote work aids organizational strategy and is willing to innovate work processes, while the other selects teleworkers to create minimal disruption to the organization. The strategic users tend to value flexibility

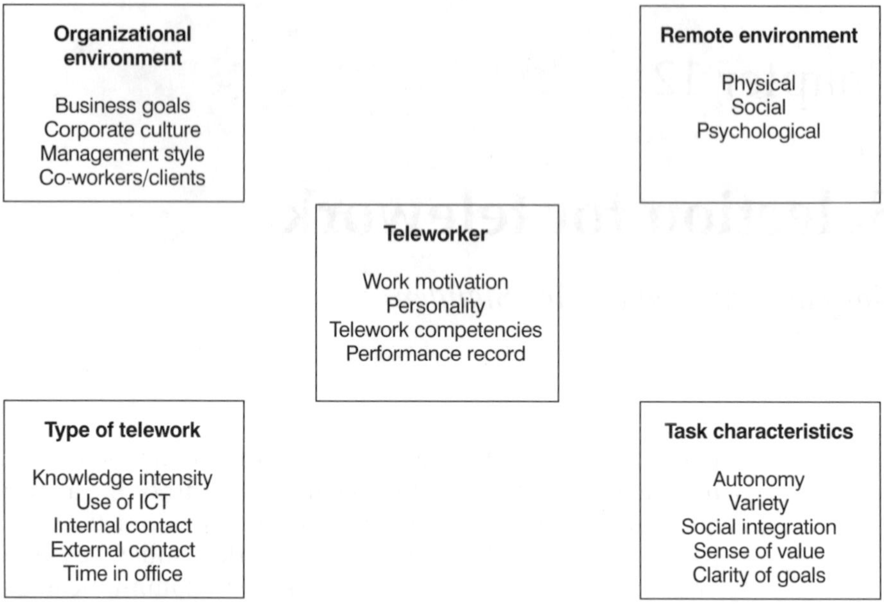

FIGURE 12.1   Variables in teleworker selection

over rules and procedures, and to consider the psychological and social consequences of telework.

What effective firms possess is not so much in-depth knowledge or a specific technical approach, but a systemic view of selection based on three principles. First, the role of telework in achieving the organization's purpose is clear; telework is not a response to a narrow problem, nor a faddish trend copied from other organizations. Second, telework is an attempt to jointly optimize the organization's social and technical systems. Neither computer systems nor management systems can be fully effective unless integrated with the social system (Trist *et al.*, 1963; Taylor, 1987). How remote workers will maintain relations with colleagues, superiors and social networks, as well as their involvement in corporate culture, is very important. Third, individual preferences concerning the social and technical aspects of remote work must be considered. Researchers have shown that employees perform better when job satisfaction, quality of working life and psychological well-being are not compromised (Hackman and Oldham, 1980; Warr, 1987), and studies of teleworkers show how the different preferences and goals of individuals contribute to these outcomes (e.g. Ramsower, 1985; Bailyn, 1989). If, for example, teleworkers feel uncomfortable without immediate feedback on their work, or feel they cannot obtain clarity about management goals, they may be better off in an office.

These three principles – addressing business goals, maintaining the social system and working with individual preferences – should determine the involvement of variables such as those in Figure 12.1 in selection. We now examine the individual components of Figure 12.1.

Type of telework

Telework is not an all-or-none phenomenon but an array of practices varying on ICT usage, knowledge intensity, intra- and extra-organizational contact, and location (see Daniels *et al.*, Chapter 1). This implies that there is not an 'ideal teleworker' but rather that different types of individuals may be suited to different forms of telework. For example, the need for self-discipline, self-organization, independent work and effective communication vary according to the communication requirements of the task, its knowledge intensity and the ICTs involved. A remote data-entry operator might have little need for such attributes and could be managed on the basis of outputs. On the other hand, certain professionals may be assumed to have independent work skills and these would not be specifically targeted in teleworker selection. For all sorts of workers, communication skills are less important if they regularly visit the office. The important point is to select according to the specific type rather than some abstract concept of telework.

Another aspect of telework is whether staff are permanent or have contract or casual status. In this chapter we focus on permanent staff who telework either as a voluntary option or because the work requires it. For contract and casual staff, issues of employee commitment and managerial control make selection more complex, and the psychological contract between employer and worker (see Sparrow, Chapter 10) assumes greater importance.

The organizational environment

Business goals and organizational culture

In Chapter 4, Standen described the variety of business goals that telework serves, and noted that organizational cultures do not always support telework. A first step in the selection process, then, is to clarify the purpose of telework and hence the scope of the process. A second is to examine whether organizational cultures pose limits for teleworker selection: telework may not succeed if it goes against the work unit's culture. Further, as teleworkers may have less contact with the social systems that reinforce commitment to goals, it is important to select teleworkers whose values are congruent with those of the organizational unit (see Billsberry, Chapter 5).

Management style

Successful telework requires supervisors and managers who are able to work with the arrangement (see Lamond, Chapter 11), and hence these are in a sense 'selected'. Two distinct reactions to telework can be found. Some supervisors and managers find communication difficulties make teleworkers harder to manage (Ramsower, 1985), while others say teleworkers are easier to manage, since focusing on outputs rather than process reduces the need for continuous surveillance (Quaid and Lagerberg, 1992). Indeed, this focus leads some to report that having teleworkers actually improves their ability to manage (Frolick *et al.*, 1992).

Ideal attributes for telework managers include a high level of trust, good communication skills and the ability to manage by outcomes rather than micromanaging the work process. Good telework managers are often seen as facilitators rather than controllers, and need to be emotionally sympathetic to employees. Managers should also feel that their own status and credibility are not in question because their staff are not in the office – some feel their image as a manager depends on being seen to have people and activities around them. Finally, a good understanding of what it is like to be a teleworker is a useful prerequisite.

Socialization and organizational learning opportunity

The extent to which the worker's unit provides opportunities for social contact is very relevant to selection (Billsberry, Chapter 5). Social functions, training sessions and meetings not only pass on information directly related to work procedures, but also reinforce organizational values and provide an opportunity for informal learning from peers, subordinates and superiors. These features augur well for remote work, and should be included in the selection process.

Impact on colleagues and clients

Some studies have found that telework has a negative effect on the worker's colleagues, decreasing communication and cohesion (Ramsower, 1985) or productivity (Quaid and Lagerberg, 1992). Equally, there are studies showing no negative effects (Heilman, 1988), and reports of improved relations with co-workers (Olson, 1987; Dubrin, 1991). Factors such as the type of work, the use of ICTs and the extent of office visits may partly account for this variability. Clearly, though, the impact on colleagues is potentially important and needs to be considered in selection. The effect on clients may also be relevant: telework may bring better client focus if it improves work quality or increases proximity to clients, but equally may be negative where communicating with clients is difficult. Home-based telework in particular also suffers from a negative image amongst the business community that may affect client perceptions of professionalism, although in many cases clients need not know where the work is done.

The remote environment

The remote work environment contains physical, social and psychological factors relevant to selection. In Chapter 9, Standen described the home/work interface in detail, and here we cover issues relevant to selection for all forms of telework.

The physical environment   For home-based telework, some organizations require an inspection of the home office to comply with health and safety standards, particularly bearing in mind responsibilities in compensation and insurance claims (see Daniels, Chapter 8). In other arrangements, teleworkers sign a contract certifying that a suitable office exists. At the minimum a home office should be quiet, ergonomically correct, and have adequate lighting and temperature control. Teleworkers in the field face health and safety factors that are probably familiar to human resource management staff from experience with other field workers. Telecentres may provide good physical conditions, though compliance with organizational standards cannot always be taken for granted.

The social environment   Telework brings employees into contact with people outside the organization and teleworkers need the skills to manage such contacts. In the case of nomadic workers, social relations with clients or community members can be expected to increase. For many home-based teleworkers, managing separation from the family is vital (see Standen, Chapter 9). In particular, minding children is not normally compatible with work and some telework programmes require employees to show that suitable arrangements for child or elder care exist. Conflict with spouses who find their territory or independence curtailed is another issue: the emotional support of other residents is vital and they should be included in the decision-making process. At the very least, telework candidates should have discussed the issues at home and be prepared to indicate that they have family support.

The psychological environment   Psychological well-being, and ultimately work performance, are influenced by the worker's ability to adjust mentally to both distance from the organization and the new work context. While tests for psychological readiness for telework have not yet been developed, some general principles can be identified from studies of psychological well-being in conventional workers (Warr, 1987). Teleworkers should:

- experience variety in work conditions – spending 40 hours per week alone in one room is likely to reduce psychological well-being;
- have appropriate opportunity for work-related social contact (neither too much nor too little);
- feel sufficiently in control of their work – including working hours – and non-work factors like family roles and social relations;
- feel their value to the organization and its clients is not compromised by isolation.

Task characteristics

The factors we have just described as important to psychological well-being and performance are a product of the tasks involved as well as the remote work environment. Good tasks for telework will provide control over work, variety, social integration and a sense of value to the organization. They should also have clear goals and allow the worker to use their skills.

From a management perspective, tasks suited to telework should not require a great deal of direct supervision, either because workers have a high degree of autonomy or because measurable outcomes exist. Beyond this, specific advice depends on the type of telework, as we will illustrate in relation to two of the five dimensions noted by Daniels *et al.* in Chapter 1.

First, both knowledge-intense and routine jobs are suited to telework, though in different ways. Knowledge-intense teleworkers include accountants, architects, lawyers, managers, professionally trained consultants, technicians, surveyors, draftspersons, journalists, teachers, graphic designers, researchers and information systems workers. In contrast to some perceptions, a fair proportion of telework could be described as managerial – in one survey this included more than 20 per cent of telework jobs (Omari, 1999). Managerial telework is not restricted to administrative work such as reading and writing reports: remote management is possible, even for substantial periods, as long as communication and team cohesion are sustained.

A common element in knowledge-based jobs suited to home or telecentre-based telework is a need for independent thought and a high degree of concentration. Tasks such as reading, report writing, analysis, research, and planning are prime candidates. Some authorities suggest that creative work is also suitable (Gray *et al.*, 1993), although at times creativity may require contact as much as isolation. Another element that predisposes knowledge-intense jobs to telework is the high level of employee autonomy that usually accompanies them, although other workers may be equally capable of self-direction but are given less scope for it in conventional work.

Jobs relying less on formal knowledge that are suited to telework include manufacturing or craftwork, word processing, data entry, sales and marketing, customer service, book-keeping, property management, insurance claims, telephone work and business consulting. These jobs may be teleworked for a variety of reasons: to reduce office or travel costs, to improve employee recruitment, or because the work is better done in the field. In most cases, measurable outcomes are a key requirement.

A second variable that makes tasks suited to telework is the degree of internal and external contact they involve. What is important is not so much the amount of contact as the extent to which it can be achieved through ICTs, or visits to the office or clients' premises. For example, high-contact telephone-based work is well suited to telework, as the world-wide growth of remote call centres shows. Indeed, high contact work is considered more successful by some teleworkers, since it provides more feedback and keeps the teleworker involved in the organization (Omari, 1999). It is also relevant to consider whether contact is needed during or outside business hours, and whether it needs to be synchronous (both parties communicate at the same time) – perhaps asynchronous media such as e-mail or voicemail have advantages.

The person

Telework motivation

The reasons for seeking remote work have a strong bearing on its success in home or telecentre-based arrangements, which are usually voluntary. Research on home-based workers shows that many have good reasons for preferring telework and will work hard to keep it. Women most commonly seek to resolve the significant constraints imposed by child or elder care, while men, and women without children, are motivated by work-related goals such as achieving greater concentration, or aim to balance work and leisure (Blake and Suprenant, 1990; Omari, 1999). Most teleworkers are also attracted to the greater independence and control over work.

A recent study of home-based teleworkers has shown how motivations are related to life and career stage (Omari, 1999). Older workers had fewer family obligations and were more interested in the physical fitness opportunities afforded by telework. Married workers tended to be more advanced in their careers than single people and were attracted by the intrinsic rewards of the work such as greater productivity, creativity and avoidance of office distractions. Better educated teleworkers were less motivated by reduced commuting than by intrinsic or lifestyle rewards.

The distinction between intrinsic and instrumental orientation to work (Bailyn, 1989) is useful here. Successful teleworkers often find the work is *intrinsic*ally satisfying; they are rewarded by achieving goals, improving quality, learning new procedures and so on. Employees for whom work is *instrumental* in achieving other goals such as status, socialization or career progression may find remote work a problem since it reduces their visibility and participation in organizational networks. Some may be willing to put aside their instrumental goals if telework is the only option for employment, as women seeking home-based work to meet care obligations have done. The precise consequences for one's career depend, of course, on whether telework is temporary or permanent, full-time or part-time, and on the labour market status of the job. Invisibility especially affects those in less secure positions, such as women in clerical or administrative roles. Potential teleworkers with instrumental goals should be made aware of these problems.

Other specific reasons for seeking home or telecentre-based work include difficulty in commuting, spouse relocation, desire to live in rural areas, shortage of local employment opportunities, illness and disability. Despite this diversity of motives, some organizations still allow telework only as a home-based option for women with children, stereotyped thinking that limits an organization's flexibility. The selection process should recognize that many reasons for preferring not to work in an office, including the personality issues discussed next, indicate potential gains in teleworker performance and satisfaction.

Personality

Personality influences the reasons for seeking home or telecentre-based work and its success (see also, Lamond, Chapter 7). Teleworking professionals are often strongly motivated by achievement (Olson, 1989; Omari, 1999), striving hard to improve their performance and setting high goals. Omari found they tend to have a high need for autonomy and less need to dominate others, to belong to the organizational group or to achieve status. Autonomy over the physical environment of work was also important. These workers had a strong work ethic but little regard for rules and regulations that hampered their freedom. This ethic has obvious advantages as long as staff stay in touch with organizational expectations.

At the same time Omari's study contradicted the stereotype of teleworkers as introverted and conservative individuals. Most described themselves as outgoing, venturesome and flexible people who met their social needs during periods in the office, via the telephone or e-mail, or else away from work. While some forms of telework are attractive to introverted individuals, extroverts who can get their needs met are equally suited.

It is interesting that teleworkers in Omari's study reported that believing in the job was important to success. Psychologists have found that work gives meaning to life through factors such as feedback from supervisors, friendships with colleagues, and opportunities for asserting one's individuality or status (e.g., Hackman and Oldham, 1980; Warr, 1987). Lacking these opportunities, teleworkers need to find meaning in the value of their contribution to the organization or its clients.

Teleworkers in routine occupations may be less driven by achievement but can find other aspects of telework satisfying, particularly autonomy over work schedules and the physical environment and greater responsibility for outcomes. Where they do not derive much meaning from the work, the ability to balance work and non-work goals may be a strong attraction.

Personality can be assessed in the selection process through psychometric tests, ensuring that telework jobs are filled by individuals with appropriate needs and motivations. Lamond further examines the personality types and traits that are suited to different forms of telework in Chapter 7.

Distance working competencies

Commonly cited competencies for remote work include self-discipline, organization skills, communication skills, self-direction, negotiation skills and capacity for self-assessment (Kinsman, 1987; Gray et al., 1993). Omari (1999) found that success in telework was also related to tough mindedness, trusting others, being assertive, being practical, basing decisions on facts and being flexible. Together these competences indicate a low need to be supervised by, to check up on, or to get help from others. For those able to set their own work hours the ability to balance work with other activities is important as teleworkers are prone to overwork (Olson, 1989; Omari, 1999). Although these competencies are not always readily incorporated in the selection process (Sparrow and Daniels, 1999), they may have positive effects on productivity and well-being.

Performance record

Not surprisingly, employees with good performance records are better candidates for remote work (Kinsman, 1987; Omari, 1999). There is some debate, however, over whether teleworkers need to be the best performers, with one author suggesting that the best candidates may be those for whom telework can *improve* performance (Filipczak, 1992). New employees, those in the early stages of a career, or those returning to work are not eligible in many schemes. Other aspects of a candidate's work history that suggest difficulties are absenteeism, psychological conditions related to stress, and problems with food, alcohol or drug abuse.

Developing a selection process

We have discussed a comprehensive list of factors that could form the basis of a selection protocol aimed at ensuring that teleworkers have skills and preferences suited to the task, the organizational context and the remote environment. The appendix to this chapter shows the kinds of issues addressed in selecting teleworkers in one large private sector organization, although their relevance to any other specific organization is not guaranteed. Further insight on how to fit the worker to the job and the organization is found in Billsberry's discussion in Chapter 5.

Telework is superficially attractive to many employees – perhaps half of those in a typical office – but its true nature can be quite different to expectations. A formal selection process should therefore include an information package covering issues such as social isolation and involvement in corporate culture, personality types, work competencies and regulations on health and safety. Other topics include setting up a remote workstation or office, role conflict, teleworker and supervisor responsibilities, ICT issues, impact on client contact, valid types of work, overwork and the career consequences of reduced visibility. Information sheets and checklists for colleagues and household members may also be useful. Some firms have devised contracts that specify the hours and location of remote work, reporting arrangements and such aspects of the home environment as child care arrangements and social separation. The important point is that applicants for remote work have a realistic understanding of it, including the viewpoints of supervisors, colleagues, and family if relevant.

Equity issues should also be canvassed, as teleworkers can be advantaged or disadvantaged compared to conventional workers. *Ad hoc* telework arrangements may create perceptions of favouritism and are often not widely publicized. If the benefits and conditions of teleworkers are different to those of office workers, lowered morale can result. Finally, teleworkers' reduced visibility may affect their career, particularly where low status or a 'glass ceiling' is also disadvantageous. The selection interview might cover a candidate's awareness of visibility and strategies for maintaining it.

Finally, we note that some deficiencies in an individual's suitability can be remedied by training in areas such as self-management (Salmon *et al.*,

Chapter 14), by use of appropriate technology (Harper, Chapter 6), by a suitable performance management system (van Ommeren, Chapter 15) or by the provision of additional organizational support. Teleworkers do not have to be perfect.

Conclusion

As telework breaks through the neat though ultimately artificial walls of the 9 to 5 office regime, it inevitably makes selection more complex. One answer is to use a systemic approach to work through a broad range of variables such as those in Figure 12.1. We suggest three systemic principles: relating telework to the organization's goals; considering how it affects both the technical system and the social system; and matching employees personalities, preferences and skills to both systems. The five components of Figure 12.1 should operate harmoniously in pursuit of business goals.

We have seen that general criteria for teleworkers such as Kinsman's (1987) self-discipline, good organizational skills, job commitment, capacity for independent work and effective communication are relevant in many cases, though less so for routine workers or tasks heavily dependent on technology. Equally, general guidelines for the type of task suited to telework need to be seen in the light of the worker's motivation, personality and competencies: some people want autonomy and social contact in work, others do not. Further, the value of general guidelines looks set to decline as telework evolves: more effective technology and other factors will bring a wider range of jobs, workers and remote environments. Even if these changes are incremental rather than revolutionary, we can expect that in the future managers will increasingly use a systemic approach to teleworker selection.

References

Bailyn, L. (1989) Towards the perfect workplace. *Communications of the Association for Computing Machinery,* **32**, 460–71.

Blake, V.L.P. and Suprenant, T.T. (1990) Electronic immigrants in the information age: public policy considerations. *The Information Society,* **7**, 233–44.

Dubrin, A. (1991) Comparison of the job satisfaction and productivity of telecommuters versus in-house employees: A research note on work in progress. *Psychological Reports,* **68**, 1223–34.

Filipczak, B. (1992) Telecommuting: a better way to work? *Training,* May, 53–61.

Frolick, M.N., Wilkes R.B. and Urwiler, R. (1993) Telecommuting as a workplace alternative: an identification of significant factors at home in American firms' determination of work-at-home policies. *Journal of Strategic Information Systems,* **2**, 206–22.

Gray, M., Hudson, N. and Gordon, G. (1993) *Teleworking Explained.* Chichester: Wiley.

Hackman, J.R. and Oldham, G. (1980) *Work Redesign.* Reading, MA: Addison-Wesley.

Heilman, W. (1988) The organizational development of teleprogramming. In W.B. Korte, S. Robinson and W.J. Steinle (eds) *Telework: Present situation and Future Development of a New Form of Work Organization.* Amsterdam: Elsevier.

Kinsman, F. (1987) *The Telecommuters*. New York: Wiley.

Olson, M.H. (1987) Telework: practical experience and future prospects. In R.E. Kraut (ed.) *Technology and the Transformation of White Collar Work*. Hillsdale, NJ: Erlbaum.

Olson, M.H. (1989) Work at home for computer professionals: current attitudes and future prospects. *Association for Computing Machinery Transaction on Office Information Systems*, **7**, 317–38.

Omari, M. (1999) *The Ideal Homeworkers: An Investigation of Personal and Job Requirements for Successful Home-based Work*. Unpublished thesis for the degree of Master of Business (Human Resource Management), Edith Cowan University.

Quaid, M. and Lagerberg, B. (1992) Puget Sound Telecommuting Demonstration. Washington State Energy Office: WSEO Publication 92–138.

Ramsower, R.M. (1985) *Telecommuting: The Organizational and Behavioral Effects of Working at Home*. Ann Arbor, Michigan: UMI Research Press.

Senge, P. (1990) *The Fifth Discipline: The Art and Practice of the Learning Organization*. New York: Doubleday.

Sparrow, P.R. and Daniels, K. (1999) Human resource management in the virtual organization. In C.L. Cooper and S.E. Jackson (eds) *Trends in Organizational Behavior*. Volume 5. Chichester: Wiley.

Taylor, J. (1987) Job design and the quality of working life. In R. Kraut (ed.) *Technology and the Transformation of White Collar Work*. Hillsdale, NJ: Erlbaum.

Trist, E.L., Higgin, G.W., Murray, H. and Pollock, A.B. (1963) *Organizational Choice: Capabilities of Groups at the Coal Face Under Changing Technologies: The Loss, Rediscovery and Transformation of a Work Tradition*. London: Tavistock Publications.

Warr, P. (1987) *Work, Unemployment and Mental Health*. Oxford: Oxford University Press.

Appendix   Checklist from a large private sector organization

Employee considerations

- Why do you want to work off-site?
- What elements of your job can be performed off-site?
- How will you and your manager measure your performance?
- How and when will you do the work?
- Where will you do the work?
- What tools and equipment do you need to do the work?
- How will the company recover the costs of equipment?
- Do both your manager and colleagues agree with the concept of off-site work?
- Do you have appropriate dependant care in place whilst you are working?
- Does your household understand and support the arrangement?
- How will your colleagues and work flow be affected?
- Do you have a proven track record with the company?
- Do you have a good working relationship with your manager and colleagues?
- Do you have excellent negotiation and communication skills?
- Do you have a good social network outside the office?
- Are you willing to take responsibility for getting the job done?
- Can you cope with having to return to your usual place of work if required at any time by your manager?

Management considerations

- Which elements of the job can be done off-site?
- How will you and the employee measure performance?
- Is there a business reason for the arrangement?
- Are the technology, equipment, furnishings and space suitable at the off-site location?
- Is the arrangement economically viable?
- Can you cover all due diligence issues: security, insurance, award/agreement provisions?
- Does the employee have appropriate work attitudes and personal attributes?
- Does the employee have suitable dependant care arrangements?
- What methods will you and the employee use to communicate?
- How will you ensure that the employee still feels part of the team?
- How frequently will the employee attend the office and where will they work whilst there?
- What training does the employee require?
- What training or advisory support do you need to assist with the process?
- What effect will equipment breakdown have on the productivity of the off-site employee and on the work flow?

Chapter 13

Organizational learning

Olga Tregaskis and Kevin Daniels

It is now widely accepted that speed of innovation is a key source of competitive advantage (Stalk, 1988), especially as more industries exhibit the characteristics of hyper-competition (D'Aveni, 1995). The speed of innovation is partly dependent on the speed of organizational learning – how fast organizational members can learn from their experience, and pass this learning on to other organizational members. But organizational success is not simply dependent on speed if innovations can be easily imitated. It is also dependent on developing knowledge that cannot easily be duplicated by competitors (Grant, 1995). Often this knowledge is not made explicit, but instead resides in day-to-day organizational processes, activities of organizational members and the organizational culture (Walsh and Ungson, 1991). This presents a problem for managing teleworkers – the richness of face-to-face communication and collective organizational activities are often missing for teleworkers. This could easily slow the learning process, and confine it to explicit and easily communicated (and hence duplicated) knowledge. At the same time, it presents an opportunity: ICTs allow teleworkers to be connected over huge geographical distances – allowing access to diverse sources of expertise that may enhance learning. The challenge then is to find ways of managing the process of organizational learning at a distance, to ensure that innovation is timely and not easily imitated. Or put another way:

> ... the organizing processes needed for many contemporary markets mean that organizations cannot simply undertake the same old tasks at a distance (Jackson, 1997, p. 5)

The purpose of this chapter then is to identify the characteristics of organizational learning, barriers to successful learning and some of the strategies for facilitating learning in organizations with teleworkers.

The process of organizational learning

One of the earliest and most widely known frameworks for organizational learning is that proposed by Argyris and Schön (1978). They argue that organizational learning is achieved through mastering both single- and double-loop learning. Single-loop learning is achieved through the process of *error-detection–correction* resulting in incremental performance improvements. This is the most prevalent approach to learning in organizations and tackles problems at the superficial symptomatic level. Double-loop learning addresses the underlying causes of the problem. This is achieved when individuals question and review the accepted norms and operating assumptions of the company. In other words, managerial decisions and direction are challenged on a regular basis to allow organizations to recognize when to make shifts in the way thing are done rather than merely continuing to improve the current mode of working. The ability to anticipate and shift to another way of working is a vital part of organizational survival. To achieve single and double-loop learning, organizations need to develop appropriate learning cultures and climates to promote questioning of assumptions, sharing of responsibilities, and making views of the organization explicit (Argyris, 1976; Argyris and Schön, 1978).

Similarly, Senge (1990) emphasizes the organization's ability to learn and unlearn on a continual basis. Senge concentrates on the role of the individual in the learning process and the qualities that individuals need to develop within them to think and function in a learning mode. Such qualities include: ongoing appraisal of progress toward personal goals; questioning current and developing new cognitive models of the business and social environment of the organization; and ability for team members to build on each others' strengths. Like Argyris and Schön (1978), he emphasizes the importance of shared visions and the need to make assumptions explicit if people are to work toward common goals.

Brown and Duguid (1991) examine the links between work, learning and innovation in practice. They think of organizations as communities: people learning in the context of their work environment, creating communities-of-practice. Within such communities, the learning is often implicit. For individuals to learn the implicit as well as the explicit skills required, they need to be granted access to and membership of the community. Once within the community, knowledge travels fast across group members, allowing rapid response to changes in the environment. Through their focus on the continual adaptation of work to environmental demands, these communities contextualize learning and hence innovation, adapting work to the situation rather than adopting practices which are incompatible with the environment.

These explanations of organizational learning highlight the role of rapid and contextualized communication; shared visions and cultures; inclusion of individuals in 'communities'; the complexities of unravelling and learning implicit information; and the ability to question and change assumptions about working practices. For organizations with teleworkers this raises a number of significant concerns. The remainder of this chapter examines some of the barriers to organizational learning, and the strategies that can be used to overcome these barriers, in relation to teleworkers. These barriers (individual, managerial and organizational) and facilitation strategies (technical, managerial and organizational) are summarized in Figure 13.1.

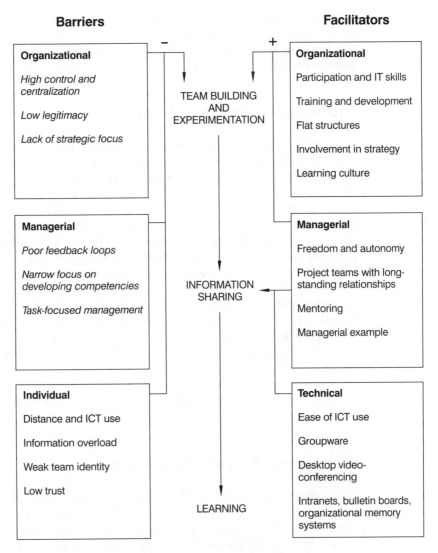

Barriers   **Facilitators**

Organizational

High control and centralization

Low legitimacy

Lack of strategic focus

TEAM BUILDING AND EXPERIMENTATION

Organizational

Participation and IT skills

Training and development

Flat structures

Involvement in strategy

Learning culture

Managerial

Poor feedback loops

Narrow focus on developing competencies

Task-focused management

INFORMATION SHARING

Managerial

Freedom and autonomy

Project teams with long-standing relationships

Mentoring

Managerial example

Individual

Distance and ICT use

Information overload

Weak team identity

Low trust

LEARNING

Technical

Ease of ICT use

Groupware

Desktop video-conferencing

Intranets, bulletin boards, organizational memory systems

FIGURE 13.1   Barriers and facilitators in organizational learning

Barriers to learning

Distance and the use of ICTs (information and communication technologies) are perhaps the most obvious barriers to learning amongst teleworking organizations. ICTs cannot capture the same richness and detail of information as face-to-face communication, nor the sense of being in the same workspace as others – hence the transfer of knowledge amongst teleworkers becomes problematic (Jackson, 1997). This situation may become less problematic in the future for reasons detailed below, though it is not likely to disappear entirely in the foreseeable future. However, these are not the only barriers to learning – in addition, teleworking organizations face many barriers also found in organizations with more traditional work processes, often intensified by the added distance. These barriers can be divided into those most closely associated with individual behaviour, managerial behaviour and organizational systems and processes.

Individual barriers to learning

ICTs can lead to problems of information overload (see Daniels, Chapter 8). To cope with this, teleworkers may simply begin to ignore communications from others. Ultimately, if they screen out too much information, they may not get a feel for how other team members work, and may not see themselves as part of a team but rather as individual workers (Jackson, 1997). This mindset may lead to further failure to communicate with team members on a regular basis, as communication is thought of as less relevant to the task in hand – reinforcing the perception of individual workers rather than a team. ICTs also allow teleworkers to become members of several teams, typically crossing functional boundaries, and sometimes even organizational boundaries as contract workers, suppliers or customers join the virtual team. This may also weaken team identity and lessen the perceived need for communication. Moreover, it can lead to teleworkers having conflicts of interest amongst teams, and weaken the trust team members have in each other (Townsend *et al.*, 1998). As face-to-face contact might be limited, it is also more difficult to build trust. Together, these issues may influence teleworkers to stop sharing information and questioning assumptions. Beyond the difficulties in providing rich and detailed information, the problems then are those of information overload, building trust, team identity and communication.

Managerial barriers to learning

The remote nature of teleworking means that managers need to place a strong emphasis on finding ways of engaging teleworkers in the wider organizational community. The degree of learning that individual teleworkers experience on the job may be significant. Under office-based conditions a number of forums exist for that knowledge to be transferred to colleagues. However, this may not happen with teleworkers and consequently the flow of information back into the organization is hindered.

Teleworkers, like other employees, need attention paid to personal development needs. Too often teleworkers are viewed within the context of a specific project and, as such, managers may consider that experience addresses their development needs. Alternatively, teleworkers are considered to have expert knowledge and are given projects in keeping with this knowledge. It is important to recognize the need to develop wider sets of competencies that go beyond current job requirements. If the wider potential of the teleworker is ignored, then the organization is not utilizing its resources fully.

A further issue, which is particularly problematic for teleworkers, is that teleworking is most often managed by outputs, and management is often task focused. This particular approach is not conducive to organizational learning (Jackson, 1997). It prevents managers and teleworkers from seeing connections amongst tasks, and how those connections can be enhanced to build better formal and informal communication amongst teleworkers.

The managerial barriers to learning in essence are linked to the very limited perceptions of the role of teleworkers (i.e. the tasks and projects which are appropriate for them) and the lack of an active approach to managing such workers for wider organizational benefits.

Organizational barriers to learning

At the organizational level the adoption of telework can be viewed as a response to changes in technology. For example, the introduction of technology such as local area networks (LANs) represents one organization-wide reason for adopting telework. At the same time, teleworking challenges conventional ways of working and has implications for the organization's culture, structure and strategy. Unless cultural, structural and strategic issues are addressed, organizational and individual learning can be severely hampered. In *cultural* terms, teleworking needs to be seen to be a legitimate form of working. Cultures give signals to employees about how things are done and behaviours which are valued and those which are not (see also Standen, Chapter 4). This is reinforced by, for example, the organization's performance management system. Teleworkers and teleworking are often seen as peripheral, yet may contribute to the core competencies of the business. The organizational culture therefore needs to signal the value of this form of working to both teleworkers themselves and wider organizational members. In terms of the *organizational structure* certain approaches will be more appropriate than others. To some extent this depends on the level of teleworking within the organization and how it relates to other forms of working. High levels of centralized decision making and control are not conducive to the learning amongst workers in general. This is particularly true for teleworkers because the nature of the ICTs prevents the rich but subtle and implicit information about organizations that is transmitted in the decision-making process. At the *strategic* level the utilization of teleworkers and the role they play in achieving wider organizational objectives should be considered. As with any other form of flexible working, without this perspective, the organization has no mechanism for feeding learning back into strategy, or into any of the more general organizational learning processes.

In essence, learning capability is likely to be lost or stifled where the wider organizational infrastructure does not support this mode of working (see Lamond, Chapter 3 and Standen, Chapter 4).

Facilitating learning processes

There are several sets of strategies that can be used to overcome these barriers to organizational learning and, indeed, to enhance learning directly. These strategies can be divided into technical, managerial and organizational. We will discuss each of these strategies in turn.

Technical facilitators

Developments in ICTs can help provide richer and more detailed information, prevent information overload and build teams. Although better ICTs can help people share information, they cannot *make* people share information unless proper managerial and organizational supports exist. Nor will ICTs have a great impact on organizational learning unless they are easy to use (Townsend *et al.*, 1998). For example, video-conferencing that is as easy to use as the telephone may help the transmission of rich, detailed and informal information much better than a video-conference that needs a special room, which has to be booked some time beforehand.

Developments in groupware and desktop video-conferencing can help teleworkers share rich and detailed information (Boudreau *et al.*, 1998; Townsend *et al.*, 1998; see also Harper, Chapter 6). Groupware such as Lotus Notes allows real-time electronic messaging, screen sharing, group scheduling, group writing and group brainstorming. Together with desktop video-conferencing, which enables more complex face-to-face communication, groupware may go some way towards imitating, if not substituting for, face-to-face group work. An important feature of the latter technology is that real-time access is not needed. This reduces information overload by allowing teleworkers access to information when they need it, rather than having to react to vast quantities of data simply because they are there. Such systems can also allow teleworkers to access rich sources of information, documented as text, audio or visual archives. Examples here include intranets with their own search engines, bulletin boards and organizational memory systems (Boudreau *et al.*, 1998). These organizational memory systems enable automatic acquisition, retention, maintenance, search and retrieval of information (Stein and Zwass, 1995). They can also be useful for team-building purposes. By examining archives to find collaborators that have been successful in the past, managers may be able to configure teams rapidly by identifying individuals that are likely to work well together and share information (Townsend *et al.*, 1998; see also De Fillippi and Arthur, 1998).

Managerial facilitators

Freedom to experiment and organize work are often key for the teleworker in finding novel or innovative solutions to problems. Traditional managerial approaches tend to organize and control this process. In reality, this is difficult to do and managers must learn to trust the judgement and methods of their colleagues, even when they are not familiar to them. Trust can be enhanced by establishing project teams where members already have long-standing relationships (cf. De Fillippi and Arthur, 1998). Less experienced team members can be allocated an experienced colleague to act as a mentor by sharing information amongst team members, teaching appropriate use of ICTs and building other learning skills. Managers too can encourage all team members to share information and enhance their learning capability by openly advocating the use of ICTs for information sharing for more than just formal communication (Boudreau et al., 1998). This can be most readily achieved by setting good examples of the appropriate media for sharing information amongst colleagues (see Johnson, 1990).

Organizational facilitators

Organizational systems that develop team participation skills and IT skills will have a benefit for organizational learning – as these skills enable teleworkers to adapt to new teams quickly and to share information readily amongst established teams (Townsend et al., 1998). Such skills can be trained, or people who already possess these skills can be selected (see Salmon et al., Chapter 14; and Omari and Standen, Chapter 12). However, there are wider organizational facilitators of learning embedded in structures and cultures. Jones and Hendry (1994) suggest three strategies to encourage active learning in organizations:

1   providing access to training and development (see Salmon et al.), including continual access to training on ICT developments, so that organizations can make the most of the learning capabilities afforded by developments in ICTs (Townsend et al., 1998);
2   encouraging participative management and flatter organizational structures, so that people become involved in decisions (see Lamond, Chapter 3);
3   involving people at all levels in the development of organizational strategy, to create a shared strategic vision and enhance trust amongst organizational members.

Related to this, developing a 'learning culture' will encourage people to experiment and be open about successes and failures. Schein (1992) makes a number of recommendations for developing such cultures, which we have adapted to be applicable to organizations with teleworkers:

1   Develop a belief amongst teleworkers that the organization can influence its environment, but also a recognition that strategic and organizational environments are complex and difficult to analyse.
2   Ensure that teleworkers are oriented to both the near and far future.
3   Encourage teleworkers to solve their own problems.
4   Ensure that teleworkers are aware that they have direct channels to senior managers to ask questions.
5   Ensure that senior managers trust teleworkers, and communicate this trust to teleworkers.
6   Ensure that managers recognize when teleworkers need to work individually, and when they need to work as a team.

7   Ensure that all people are networked by ICTs, that everyone is allowed to speak to everyone else, and that this is encouraged (e.g. senior managers reply to e-mail personally and promptly).
8   Encourage diversity of people and work practices in the organization – but ensure that there is communication amongst the diverse groups within the organization.

Conclusion

Building organizational capabilities in learning is a key task. As many of the same problems apply to teleworking organizations and those with traditional work practices, many of the solutions are similar. However, just as teleworking can modify the nature of the barriers to learning, it is not then possible to transfer the same strategies from traditional workers to teleworkers without some modification. This does not just entail the creative use of developments in ICTs, although this may help – rather it is important to see the problems and solutions in a systemic manner (Jackson, 1997, 1998). An integrated approach, involving multiple layers of analysis, may help to develop such thinking. We have presented such an approach here. However, it is also necessary for solutions to be tailored to the specific context of individual teleworkers and the organization (Jackson, 1997, 1998). The best way to achieve this might be a participatory approach to learning, in which managers involve teleworkers in decisions on the best ways to build learning capability. This requires allowing managers the time to facilitate learning and involve teleworkers in the process. It also implies allowing teleworkers time to learn and to communicate. Failure may lead to marginalization of teleworkers in the learning process.

References

Argyris, C. and Schön, D. (1978) *Organizational Learning: A Theory of Action Perspective.* Wokingham: Addison-Wesley.

Argyris, C. (1976) Single-loop and double-loop models in research on decision making. *Administrative Science Quarterly*, **21**, 363–77.

Boudreau, M.C., Loch, K.D., Robey, D. and Straud, D. (1998) Going global: using information technology to advance the competitiveness of the virtual transnational organization. *Academy of Management Executive*, **12**, November, 120–8.

Brown, J.S. and Duguid, P. (1991) Organizational learning and communities-of-practice: toward a unified view of working, learning, and innovation. *Organization Science*, **2**, 40–57.

D'Aveni, R.A. (1995) Coping with hyper competition: utilizing the new 7 S's framework. *Academy of Management Executive*, **9**, August, 45–60.

DeFillippi, R.J. and Arthur, M.B. (1998) Paradox in project-based enterprise: the case of film making. *California Management Review*, **40**, 125–39.

Grant, R.M. (1995) *Contemporary Strategy Analysis: Concepts, Techniques, and Applications.* Oxford: Blackwell.

Jackson, P.J. (1997) Flexibility and rigidity in new forms of work: individual versus organizational issues. Presented at the Congress of the European Association of Work and Organizational Psychologists, Verona, Italy, April.

Jackson, P.J. (1998) Integrating the teleworking perspective into organizational analysis and learning. In P.J. Jackson and J.M. Van der Wielen (eds) *Teleworking: International Perspectives, From Telecommuting to the Virtual Organization*. London: Routledge.

Johnson, G. (1990) Managing strategic change: the role of symbolic action. *British Journal of Management*, **1**, 183–200.

Jones, A.M. and Hendry, C. (1994) The learning organization: adult learning and organizational transformation. *British Journal of Management*, **5**, 153–62.

Schein, E.H. (1992) *Organizational Culture and Leadership* (2nd edn) San Francisco: Jossey Bass.

Senge, P.M. (1990) *The Fifth Discipline*. London: Doubleday.

Stalk, G. (1988) Time – the next source of competitive advantage. *Harvard Business Review*, July–August, 41–51.

Stein, E.W. and Zwass, V. (1995) Actualizing organizational memory with information systems. *Information Systems Research*, **6**, 85–117.

Townsend, A.M., DeMarie, S. and Hendrickson, A.R. (1998) Virtual teams: technology and the workplace of the future. *Academy of Management Executive*, **12**, August, 17–29.

Walsh, J.P. and Ungson, G.R. (1991) Organizational memory. *Academy of Management Review*, **16**, 41–51.

Chapter 14

Training and development for online working

Gilly Salmon, John Allan and Ken Giles

The focus of this chapter is on the need to train and develop teleworkers. The strengths and weaknesses of various media for training and developing are considered. By way of illustration, a case study is offered of the development, implementation and evaluation of an initiative to meet the training and development needs of a group of teleworkers.

Introduction

Out of sight should never be out of mind where the training and development of teleworkers is concerned. It forms part of an organization's overall human resource strategy. To echo Harrison:

> Employee development as part of the organization's overall human resource strategy means the skilful provision and organization of learning experiences in the workplace in order that performance can be improved, that work goals can be achieved and that ... there can be continuous organizational as well as individual growth. (1992, p. 4)

An approach to the training and development for teleworkers needs to go beyond narrow skills of using a particular piece of software or of following a particular routine. There are many areas of potential benefit. Corporate values and mission, communication skills, teleworkers' location in internal and external customer supply chains, self and time management, health and safety requirements for off-site working, company security policy, legal, tax and insurance requirements of homeworking, technical skills of using hardware and software – all are examples of potential areas to add value through training and development. Counsellors, career advisers, coaches and mentors, line managers and online support services may also become involved in matters that are often classified as training and development issues. Human resource managers should also consider targeting telework managers and the colleagues of teleworkers. All such people may need to understand company policy, the practicalities of telework, the motivation of teleworkers and how to maintain communication and support networks.

Media for training teleworkers

What follows assumes that a strategy is already in place to identify teleworkers' training and development needs and that 'what is needed and why?' has been clarified. Given this, the circumstances of teleworking mean that there is a rich array of potential media resources to be considered as part of a planned approach to answering the questions 'how, when and where?' In Table 14.1, we offer some suggestions and indicate some of the potential advantages and disadvantages. These can be expanded to take account of particular circumstances and experience. The choice of medium should be one that suits the individual learner and does not cause a 'struggle to learn' (Duchastel, 1997). This is critical, as not all media offer good interactivity (Bates, 1995). (For an analysis of media for teaching see Laurillard, 1993.) These various media can also be represented on a matrix to show the extent to which they are time and location dependent (Figure 14.1).

Table 14.1 and Figure 14.1 can be used to deal with questions about the degree of dispersal of the participants and about whether the training and development would benefit from being synchronous or asynchronous. There

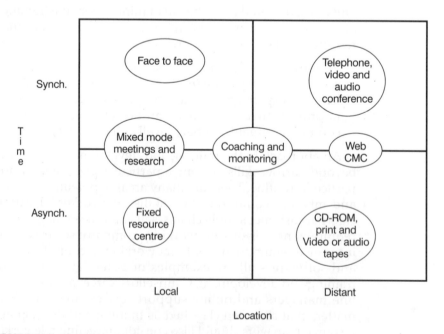

FIGURE 14.1   Synchronous/asynchronous training media matrix

TABLE 14.1 Strengths and weaknesses in choice of media for training

Medium	What is it?	Main strengths	Main weaknesses
Print	Books, leaflets	Portable, easy to use, anytime, anywhere. Easy to prepare and no set-up costs once prepared. Can be part of a multi-media approach	Lack interaction and multimedia richness. Feedback uncertain and slow, although in-text self-assessed activities and tests may be built in
Telephone	One to one or 'conference call'	Enables synchronous discussion. Agenda can be prepared in advance and feedback can be collected online	Real-time event. Lack of visual cues. Control difficult if many taking part and needs skilled handling and arrangement. An unfamiliar use of an everyday medium?
Face-to-face	One to one or group meeting	Can be highly participatory and flexible. Body language apparent. Feedback easy to obtain	Real-time event. Time, travel and organizational demands. Problem of absentees from group events. Benefits uncertain for every participant
Web	Pages on the Web, sometimes with multimedia	Easy updates. Wide choice of content	Slow. Requires access. Do in-house design skills exist?
CD-ROM	On-screen print or multimedia	Fast interaction. Multimedia. May be available off the shelf?	Not easily modifiable or updateable. Expensive to produce and requires special design skills
Audio conference	Usually via the Web	Enables synchronous discussion	Difficult to control with more than about six. Needs setting up
Computer-mediated conference (CMC)	E-mail-based conference that is moderated	Asynchronous for reflection. A written record of interaction. Guided by moderator. Feedback relatively easy	Requires access and setting up. Asynchronous interaction slow. Requires training and socialization for moderators and users to work effectively. Help desk may be needed
Video lecture	Broadband transmission	Enables lecture to reach many	No control by user. Needs setting up. Poor potential interaction
Video conference	Usually via the Web	Body language possible	Difficult to control with more than about six. Needs setting up and skills development
Coaching and mentoring	Can be face to face or remote	Individual help. Flexible	Time consuming and expensive
Video tape	Standard video tape	Can be stopped and started at will. Can be relatively cheap to produce	Inflexible. Needs appropriate equipment. Format compatibility may be a problem in some countries
Audio tape	Standard audio tape	Can be stopped or started at will	Needs a tape player (mainly in cars now!) 'Image' problem. Inflexible
Fixed resource centre	Central location with PCs, books, CD-ROMs etc.	Helpful to those without PC, video player etc.	Expensive to set up and maintain. Users have to travel to centre

are other questions that will help to narrow down the focus in choosing a particular strategy, such as:

- Does expertise for the proposed training exist in-house or must it be bought in?
- What is the training budget for the proposed activity?
- What are the available trained human resources to support the activity?
- What are the time constraints for implementation?
- Are the trainees new or existing/experienced or less experienced?
- Are they to be trained for routine or for non-routine tasks?
- Are the numbers to be trained large or small?
- Will a single medium or multi-media approach be suitable?
- Would the training best be online or off-line?
- Will new hardware or software be needed?
- What will participants' support needs be? Will prior training in use of hardware or software for training be needed and when will it be needed? (Will a help desk be needed and what hours will it be available? Will a 'Frequently asked questions' online resource help to reduce calls on a helpdesk?)
- How will the training be evaluated?

A case study in training and developing teleworkers

There are insights be gained from one particular large-scale attempt to train and develop 'teleworkers' online through a training programme, which we developed and ran successfully (Salmon, 1998). We began with the need to train a first cohort of some 150. To date, some 300 have followed the programme. The particular circumstances relate to a knowledge-based work environment where value was added to the extent that 'customers' learning was enhanced as a result of the online performance of the 'teleworkers'. The teleworkers in this instance were part-time tutors (teachers) for the UK Open University Business School (OUBS). They are usually academically qualified practising managers who work at a distance, mostly on their own but with distance support. They are home-based and produce outcomes at a distance. They and their customers (students) are scattered over the whole of Western Europe. The 'students' for whom they are responsible are themselves practising managers who are engaged in professional development in their own time. As part of the initiative, we have had to induct over 5000 students through an online training course to enable them to benefit from the online elements of their programme of study.

Computer-conferencing and e-mail form part of the study package. Tutors need to understand the rationale for using electronic media for teaching and learning purposes; to feel comfortable in using the software; to be able to communicate and teach, mediate and moderate interaction effectively online; and to be motivated to do so. For this they need careful training.

The trainees

The first cohort to be trained and developed was needed for a foundation course for a Master of Business Administration (MBA) degree that began in February 1996. Whereas the job description specified teaching online using computer-conferencing as a requirement, the person specification required only experience with Windows software and a willingness to undergo training in the use of communications software. We therefore offered training to recruit able and experienced candidates who might not have had online teaching experience. Figure 14.2 shows a rough distribution of the successful candidates' prior experience of the OUBS and of using electronic communications media, usually e-mail. Almost none had experience of using the media for the purposes we had in mind – computer-mediated conferencing (CMC).

Figure 14.2 shows the mixture of levels of experience of those whom we were to train and develop. Why we were doing so was already specified in the brief from the team that produced the course. Answering the questions as to what we needed to include in the training programme, how we were going to achieve our objectives, when and where, formed part of the process of developing the programme. It is to this that we now turn.

Developing the training – a model

Interaction between work, learning and leisure is predicted to become much more fluid (Steele, 1996). With the advent of teleworking, this notion becomes real and the role of training to work in new ways and in new online

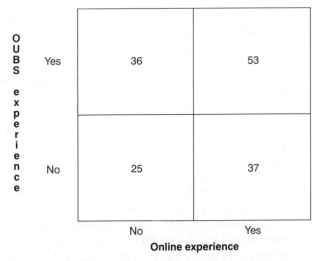

FIGURE 14.2   Previous experience of OUBS and online communications at commencement of training

environments becomes of critical importance. Moreover, there is a widening acceptance and understanding of learning as a socially mediated and constructed process (Billett, 1996) and of knowledge as no longer 'fixed' (Hendry, 1996). Therefore training to telework, especially exploiting the interactive benefits of online working, needs to take account of a much wider variety of factors than merely learning to use appropriate software. The training programme we describe had to be online, at least for early cohorts, because of the difficulties and costs of assembling the trainees in one place at the same time. The small number of suitably experienced trainers available reinforced this decision. The OUBS experience is therefore a case study that encapsulates many of the general opportunities and problems that may be encountered in training teleworkers.

We were training management tutors online to perform as moderators[1] of online conferences for students in the distance education management context. Our programme, which we saw as action research, was developed in the earliest days of training to work interactively online. In that sense it involved looking at a new problem and modelling the online experiences of early adopters and users. Feedback showed that most of the trainees enjoyed the experience of training to work online and only a few did not.

We first built a model of understanding through content analysis of voluntary use by MBA students and tutors of early online conferencing systems (Figure 14.3). We developed an understanding of the stages that users go through before becoming comfortable and competent, and move from being online novices to experts in online interaction.

Stage 1   Accessing and using the computer-mediated conferencing system

This stage involves the learner getting to know about the availability and the benefits of the CMC system, setting up his or her own system of hardware, software and password, dialling up the system and getting to the point where the conferences are available on screen. This is similar to the learning requirements of any teleworker connecting from home to a network. At the first stage of CMC use, the learner needs information and technical support to get online, and motivation to take the necessary time and effort. High motivation is a prime factor at this stage in encouraging participants to tackle the technical aspects, especially if they are dialling in from remote sites. Access to support needs to be available at the times at which the learner is likely to be struggling to get online on his or her *own*. The problem can be overcome by providing continuing encouragement and support in the form of an online 'helpdesk', a telephone helpdesk during working hours, and in some cases face-to-face advice on modem use and connection. This stage can be considered to be over at the point at which the learner posts his or her first message. Where teleworkers are concerned this critical 'set up' stage cannot be ignored and it will need to be repeated at any point that access or software is changed.

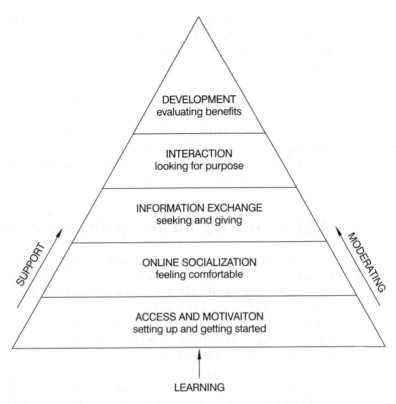

FIGURE 14.3   Model for interactive online training for teleworking

Stage 2   Becoming familiar with the online environment

Working online is a new and potentially alien world for many participants (Rowntree, 1995). From the first research on CMC, an influential discovery was the lack of expressive (i.e. non-verbal and visual) behavioural cues (Sproull and Kiesler, 1986). Some users regard this as an inadequacy that can result in a 'sense of depersonalization' (Hiltz, 1986, p. 100). Others considered the lack of face-to-face elements to be a freedom, since participants are undistracted by status and social games and can therefore 'project their personalities in written texts' (Feenberg, 1987, p. 74). Phillips and Santaro found that participants could disagree without excessive emotions or apparent clashes based on personalities and without shyer individuals having to 'fight their way in'. Some participants found it easier to ask for help online than face to face (Phillips and Santaro, 1989, p. 160). Schrum (1993, p. 171) comments that electronic connections have 'the power to transmit great emotions' and that the potential for the building of communities goes beyond the original hopes of the first electronic networkers. However, such depth and power appear not to be inevitable but to be dependent on the early experiences associated with access and then integration into the virtual community. It is therefore crucial that teleworkers are trained starting at the point when they first access the network and enabled to become 'socialized' into the cyber environment.

Much of this book points to the importance of the social aspects of teleworking. We found that this critical 'socialization' stage could not be rushed and most certainly could not be ignored for any one individual involved. When communicating face to face we can experience non-verbal language, particularly body language. In the online environment we do not have this advantage. It is very easy to cause offence or to cause misunderstanding by a badly worded message. Any training for teleworkers needs to include a session on 'netiquette' or how to behave online.

Stage 3   Asking for and giving information

It is at this stage that the users started to appreciate the broad range of information about the topics under discussion and available to them online. Information was seen to be flowing very freely and the 'cost' of responding to a request for information was low.

The messiness of conferencing was a stark contrast to well-structured and logical books, and it made demands on the participants to find what they 'really wanted'. As a result, the participants looked to the conference moderators to provide direction through the mass of data and encouragement to start using the most relevant material. Support skills related to the task focus of the group became important for moderators, as well as taking part in the processes of discovery. The interaction occurring at this stage was largely around *content* and/or sharing of information. For teleworkers, the ability to structure online material as it emerges, along with highly developed search skills, will be most necessary.

Stage 4   Collaboration – achieving purpose

At this stage the participants started to interact with each other, often in highly exposed and participative ways. The acts of formulating and writing down an idea or understanding, reading and responding to peers were seen to be a collaborative act. Once this began, it had its own momentum and power and collaborative learning could be seen to happen in very visible and often exciting ways (McConnell, 1994). At this stage, very active learning, especially the widening and appreciation of differing perspectives and understanding of application of concepts and theories, happened very obviously as conferences unfolded and developed. It is at this point in the development of learning to work online that embryonic 'communities-of-practice' can be established.

If interactive conferencing and the building of shared practice is desired through online working, the role of the conference moderator becomes important at this stage. The more successful moderators appear to demonstrate the high levels of facilitation skills related to group-building and maintenance.

Stage 5   Looking for additional benefits

At this stage, users become responsible for their own learning through the computer-mediated opportunities and need little support beyond what is already available. Learners often become most helpful as guides to newcomers to the system. This phenomenon was observed from the earliest days of large-scale conferencing (Mason, 1990). It is at this point that closed intranets and conferences can be linked to wider online systems such as the Internet with confidence that users can make appropriate use of the benefits. At this stage teleworkers may well become guides and mentors for those starting the process of learning.

Building an interactive online training programme

The principle of training online

It is 'by experiencing the learning that the meaning is constructed' (Wild, 1996, p. 139). Rowntree (1995) argues that the best way to go through the experience of learning to teach online is to begin as a learner. Although some traditional face-to-face training for specific software packages may precede or underpin the online approach, we believe that training to work online should take place through the medium itself, which has the huge advantage of being of much lower cost.

Engaging in reflective and interactive activities, especially those leading to explaining, justifying and evaluating problem solutions, is very important to learning processes. From the situated learning literature comes the notion that providing the training in context (i.e. online and within a community-of-practice) enables learning to develop as an intrinsic part of the ongoing activity (Chaiklin and Lave, 1993).

Use of metaphors

Building relationships between new and existing knowledge (Bruner, 1986) suggests careful choices both of icon and title for conferences and sections for training. The use of familiar metaphors might prove useful for explaining aspects of teleworking.

Figure 14.4, taken from OUBS online training, demonstrates simple use of metaphor. A familiar aeroplane symbol indicates the place to start and gives the sense of a journey. The drinks suggest permission to 'chat' and socialize, whereas the talking heads suggest a more serious discussion. A toolkit indicates that useful and practical techniques will be found in that conference, as well as the opportunity to build skills. The signpost suggests that there is more beyond the closed conference, but that the trainees will find directions to sources of help. We have found that clear identification of the purpose of each conference helps users to select ones that will match their needs and clearly signals the kind of communication and activity expected of participants in each conferencing area.

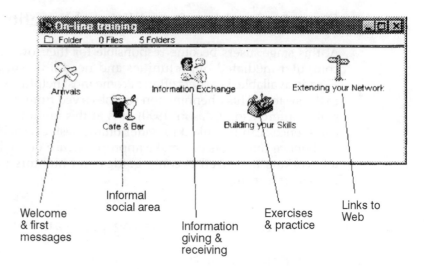

FIGURE 14.4   Use of metaphors
Screen from FirstClass Software 1999 (SoftArc. Inc., 1996).

Training structures

The metaphor of 'scaffolding' has been applied to notions of tutorial interactions between learners and teachers (Wood *et al.*, 1976). This refers to the gap between what learners can achieve alone and what they can achieve through problem solving under guidance from a teacher or in collaboration with peers (Lave and Wenger, 1991). The paradox of interactive media is that they should give greater control to the user, and yet the learner does not know enough about it to be given full control (Laurillard, 1995). Scaffolding (i.e. training by building gradually on what the learner already knows and can achieve) suggests a way of structuring this interaction and collaboration, starting with 'recruitment' of interest, establishing and maintaining an orientation towards task-relevant goals, highlighting critical features that might be overlooked, demonstrating how to achieve those goals and helping to control frustration (Wood and Wood, 1996).

The link with practice

Throughout the design processes, training designers should stay alert to the notion of training for practice, given that it would be very easy to reduce the experience to one of teaching software skills. As Rasmussen *et al.* (1991, p. 5) put it:

> To learn how to use a new medium is one matter, to learn how to integrate it into day to day practices is quite another.

It is thus necessary to build in mechanisms to ensure that users actually *take part* at each level of the training programme.

Building in reflection

People influence their everyday practice by having reflective conversations, frame their understanding of a situation in the light of experience, try out actions and then reinterpret or reframe the situation in the light of the consequences of that action (Marsick and Watkins, 1992). Through reflection the practitioner can surface and critique understandings that have grown up around a specialized practice and make sense of a situation for him or herself (Schön, 1983). To enable this to happen productively is extremely important for teleworking, since much of the informal knowledge of workers will be generated and transmitted in this way. In the early days of training, it is important to ask trainees to deliberately 'stop and reflect' by posting a message saying what they have learnt and how they can use it. This concept of reflection is crucial to online learning, and one of the critical advantages of asynchronous learning. It can also be an effective way of collecting feedback on the learner's experience of the training.

Barriers to teleworking

There are two critical barriers to online working through which trainees must pass (Figure 14.5). The barriers require techniques to enable the learner to pass to the next stage coupled with the motivation to do so. Enablement can be through suitable design that helps the learner to achieve technical ability in easy stages, and through help from online moderators. The intervention of online moderators can be highly motivating and this personal contact is an ideal method of providing the individual support that is motivating for many learners (Cornell and Martin, 1997).

The first barrier is that of learning to deal with the software that is to be used when teleworking. In some cases the teleworker may be fully familiar with all the software. In many cases, however, the software used for connection to the organization, and the e-mail software, may be new to the user. The second is the barrier to collaboration. Many teleworkers are happy

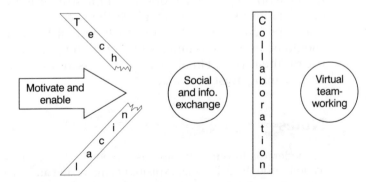

FIGURE 14.5   Barriers to teleworking

exchanging information electronically, but true collaboration, such as is required for 'virtual teams', proves very difficult without ensuring appropriate training online (Paulsen *et al.*, 1994).

It is our experience that providing instruction either face-to-face or at a distance can cross technical barriers. Where the problem is with learning how to operate connections and e-mail systems, face-to-face training is one traditional option. Where the problem is with word processing, spreadsheets, design software etc. then distance learning packages such as CD-ROMs or Internet instruction can usefully be used. There are many commercial packages available for this purpose. But online collaboration can only, in our experience, be taught online.

Evaluation

It is important, when setting up any training programme, to be explicit about what will be evaluated and how it will be done. Teleworking performance, linked to training, should be benchmarked, and training measured against the institutional or organizational standards required (MacFarlane, 1995).

Where the training has a narrow focus and outcomes are easily measured, this will not present a problem. However, at present, it is difficult to find standard models for evaluating online training for teleworking environments. For example, the Kirkpatrick model is widely cited for training evaluation (Kirkpatrick, 1959). However, this model focuses on the 'bottom line' and is based on evaluating against very specific tangible outcomes. These are unsuitable for training based on asynchronicity, reflection, learning and communities-of-practice. The design of the training programme therefore needs to recognize that the trainees will be undertaking their own interpretation and that this will occur through working with the medium and exploring this experience through and with others (Wild, 1996).

Conclusion

In this chapter, we have stressed the vital need for training and development for teleworkers. We have considered the strengths and weaknesses of a range of media for use in training, given the special circumstances of teleworking. Our experience has led us to conclude that training for online teleworkers should be provided online, using for training the very medium that they will use for their work. Finally, we have stressed that, whatever the difficulties, all such training must be evaluated.

Notes

[1] A moderator, in our definition, is someone who controls the process of communication through facilitating, explaining, organizing and structuring – in a neutral way. To be successful, moderators should be trained.

References

Bates, A.W. (1995) *Technology, Open Learning and Distance Learning*, London: Routledge.

Billett, S. (1996) Towards a model of workplace learning: the learning curriculum. *Studies in Continuing Education*, **15**, 43–57.

Bruner, J. (1986) The language of education. In J. Bruner (ed.) *Actual Minds, Possible Worlds*. Cambridge MA: Harvard University Press.

Chaiklin, S. and Lave, J. (1993) *Understanding Practice: Perspectives on Activity and Context*. Cambridge: Cambridge University Press.

Cornell, R. and Martin, B.L. (1997) The role of motivation in web-based instruction. In B.H. Khan (ed.) *Web-Based Instruction*. New Jersey: Educational Technology Publications.

Duchastel, P. (1997) A motivational framework for web-based instruction. In B.H. Khan (ed.) *Web-Based Instruction*. New Jersey: Educational Technology Publications.

Feenberg, A. (1987) Computer conferencing and the humanities. *Journal of Distance Education*, **1**, 59–70.

Harrison, R. (1992) Employee Development. London: Institute of Personnel Management.

Hendry, G. (1996) Constructivism and educational practice. *Australian Journal of Education*, **40**, 19–45.

Hiltz, S.R. (1986) The virtual classroom: using computer mediated communication for university teaching. *Journal of Communication*, **36**, 95–104.

Kirkpatrick, D.L. (1959) Techniques for evaluating training programmes. *Journal for American Society of Training Directors*, **14**, 13–18, 28–32.

Laurillard, D. (1993) *Rethinking University Teaching: A Framework for the Effective Use of Educational Technology*. London: Routledge.

Laurillard, D. (1995) Multimedia and the changing experience of the learner. *British Journal of Educational Technology*, **26**, 178–89.

Lave, J. and Wenger, E. (1991) Situated Learning. Cambridge: Cambridge University Press.

MacFarlane, A.J.G. (1995) Future patterns of teaching and learning. In T. Schuller (ed.) *The Changing University?* Milton Keynes: Open University Press.

Marsick, V. and Watkins, K.E. (1992) Continuous learning in the workplace. *Reflective Practitioner*, January, 9–12.

Mason, R. (1990) Home computing evaluation: use of computing on DT 200, 1989. Milton Keynes: Open University CITE Report 99.

McConnell, D. (1994) *Implementing Computer Supported Cooperative Learning*. London: Kogan Page.

Paulsen, M.F., Barros, B., Busch, P., Compostela, B. and Quesnel, M. (1994) A pedagogical framework for CMC programmes. In M.F. Verdejo and S.A. Cerri (eds) *Collaborative Dialogue Technologies in Distance Learning*. Berlin: Springer-Verlag.

Phillips, G.M. and Santaro, G.M. (1989) Teaching group communication via computer mediated communication. *Communication Education*, **38**, 151–61.

Rasmussen, T., Bang, J. and Lundby, K. (1991) A social experiment with electronic conferencing. *DEOSNEWS*, **1**, Issue 24.

Rowntree, D. (1995) Teaching and learning online: a correspondence education for the 21st century? *British Journal of Educational Technology*, **26**, 205–15.

Salmon, G. (1998) Developing learning through effective online moderation. *Active Learning*, December, 3–8.

SoftArc. Inc. (1996) *Global Area Communications FirstClass Client Version 3.5 for Windows*.

Schön, D. (1983) *The Reflective Practitioner: How Professionals Think in Action*. London: Basic Books.

Schrum, L. (1993) Social interaction through online writing. In R. Mason (ed.) *Computer Conferencing The Last Word*. Victoria: Beach Holme.

Sproull, L. and Kiesler, S. (1986) Reducing context cues: electronic mail in organizational communication. *Management Science*, **32**, 1492–512.

Steele, L.W. (1996) And the walls came tumbling down. *Technology in Society*, **18**, 261–84.

Wild, M. (1996) Technology refusal: rationalising the failure of student and beginning teachers to use computers. *British Journal of Educational Technology*, **27**, 134–43.

Wood, D. and Wood, H. (1996) Vygotsky, tutoring and learning. *Oxford Review of Education*, **22**, 5–15.

Wood, D.J., Bruner, J.S. and Ross, G. (1976) The role of tutoring in problem solving. *Journal of Child Psychology and Psychiatry*, **17**, 89–100.

Chapter 15

Performance management and compensation

Jos van Ommeren

Amongst the key problems faced by managers is that of assessing and managing the performance of employees. It is no less a problem for those who manage teleworkers. Indeed, it has been claimed that controlling and managing the performance of teleworkers still constitutes the major barrier to greater uptake of teleworking programmes by executives in the USA (for example, Mokhtarian and Salomon, 1996) and in Europe (IDS, 1996). The management of teleworkers' performance is the focus of this chapter.

The literature that is concerned with the management of the performance of teleworkers is small. In addition, it is frequently prescriptive and not based on consistent principles (Gordon and Kelly, 1986). In contrast, we will follow a different route. We will apply one of the most popular management theories dealing with the assessment and management of the performance of employees, 'principal agent theory' (Eisenhardt, 1989; Milgrom and Roberts, 1992), to produce a coherent and theoretically grounded approach. Principal agent theory is particularly useful when discussing management of teleworkers, since it has been developed to explain how managers may act when they are not fully able to monitor the behaviour of their subordinates.

Most authors argue that teleworking is different from other types of remote work, since teleworkers use and exchange information (Huws, 1993). Although in some contexts this may be a useful distinction, it is in general not essential to the performance management of employees who engage in telework. From the perspective of performance management, teleworking is essentially a work agreement where managers are not able directly to monitor the behaviour and, in particular, the job efforts of subordinates. As a consequence, quite apart from the usual problems of trying accurately to measure and manage employee performance, additional difficulties are encountered with respect to the assessment and management of the performance of teleworkers – 'management by walking around' does not work in the teleworking environments. Hence, managers have difficulties observing teleworkers' attendance, attitudes and appearance of working hard. As a consequence, the recommendation in the teleworking literature is to install other, more objective, measures and compensate employees based on their output, rather than their input (Johnson, 1998). Nevertheless, we will argue that it is neither always feasible nor desirable to do so, and that it may be necessary for the managers of teleworkers to rely on other tools. For this purpose, we turn to our examination of the literature on principal agent theory.

The principal agent literature

The principal agent literature focuses on work agreements between the managers (the principals) and the employees (the agents). This literature presumes that the relationship between managers and employees is not based on trust, because of differences in the objectives of managers and employees (Eisenhardt, 1989; Milgrom and Roberts, 1992). The aim of the manager is to maximize productivity at minimal cost. This aim conflicts with the objective of employees, who aim to earn as much as possible with minimal effort. It is necessary, therefore, for managers to monitor employees closely. However, it is costly for organizations to observe whether employees are engaged in productive behaviour. For example, organizations may make use of monitoring equipment, or managers may have to spend time and energy that takes them away from other necessary activities. Principal agent theory centres on ways to minimize dysfunctions in the employer–employee relationship arising out of goal conflict and information asymmetry. Of course, this description of the employer–employee relationship is quite extreme, and other approaches detailed elsewhere in this book can be useful. Nevertheless, issues of trust are problematic for teleworking (see Sparrow, Chapter 10 and Lamond, Chapter 11), and as we shall see, this extreme view is useful to help understand the core problems with performance management of teleworkers.

Beyond the question of trust and conflicting objectives, the principal agent literature concentrates mainly on three issues (Eisenhardt, 1989; Milgrom and Roberts, 1992). First, the manager may not always be able to observe directly the output and the job efforts of the employees. In other situations, the manager may observe output and/or job efforts, but only at the cost of, for example, other important managerial activities. Second, employees differ with respect to ability so that, even if employees work with maximum effort, some employees are more productive than others. The third issue relates to the recognition that the production of employees is also subject to unknown external factors.

The relevance of these issues with respect to managing subordinates depends to a large extent on the type of work considered. In some professions, output and/or effort are easily observed and monitored. For example, the output of a journalist can be easily measured, but effort is very difficult to observe, since journalists are not at their desks all of the time. In contrast, the output of managers is more difficult to measure, but effort is more easily observed. Similarly, in some jobs, differences in natural ability have a large effect on output, whilst in other work, differences in ability have a small effect on output. It is reasonable to suppose that the effect of natural ability on output becomes stronger for work that involves more problem solving and creativity, that is, more knowledge-intensive work. For example, the output of an architect is usually more closely linked to ability than, for example, data input clerks. In other situations, it is only possible to measure output of teams and not of individual employees – especially where team members' tasks are interdependent. Finally, employees often do not fully control the production they are responsible for. Sales staff can never fully control the number of items sold, and the pace of the production line is often a function of the supply of parts or the maintenance of the machinery, rather than just the efforts of the workers.

The difficulty encountered by managers is that they very often do not know fully how the output of employees depends on the behaviour and ability of the employee or on external factors. It is certainly relevant for managers to know why output is high (or low), since this will affect the compensation paid to the employees, whether promotion chances are offered etc. In addition, if performance is high because of plain good luck (for example, if there is an unusually high demand for a certain product in an area), but the employee has limited ability in sales, then the manager may wish to replace this employee with a more competent person. In other words, if the manager wishes to maximize the productivity of the employees, the manager has to decide how to design the work relationship between managers and employees, taking into account these uncertainties. We will consider here a number of ways in which managers may attempt to maximize the productivity of teleworkers.

Observing employees' behaviour

If employees have an incentive to shirk, managers may prevent shirking of employees by monitoring them. Some ways of monitoring are very straight-forward. For example, managers can easily measure whether employees work the number of hours as stipulated in the contract: managers may control whether employees arrive in time, do not take too many breaks etc. Of course, when employees work the number of hours required, this does not mean that they are more productive than those that work fewer hours. Nevertheless, one can imagine that when employees have to be at the workplace because the hours are checked, and they do not have the opportunity to engage in private activities (for example, watching television), they may choose to be productive. Managers may also observe employees' behaviour via other employees.

In the case of teleworkers, the opportunities to observe employees' behaviour by these straightforward methods are limited. This may explain why larger organizations have been found to employ fewer teleworkers than very small organizations, since very small organizations have less difficulty observing behaviour of employees in general (Barron *et al.*, 1987). This discussion does indicate the importance of information and communication technologies (ICTs) and regular meetings for contacting employees, for monitoring performance, as well as for the other reasons detailed elsewhere in this book. Nevertheless, such contact is still costly in terms of time and effort to both managers and employees.

Production, unknown external factors and performance-related compensation

Since managers are not able to monitor the behaviour of teleworkers, one solution is to evaluate output and compensate employees based on the output observed. Output control has been suggested as appropriate for a teleworking environment (Johnson, 1998). Output controls direct employees by specifying output goals and standards. In the extreme case, the income of the employees depends completely on output. In some work, this situation is not uncommon. For example, translators are often paid only in relation to the words translated. Similarly, sales persons are also often paid based on the number of products sold. Nevertheless, in many jobs, it is very difficult to measure employees' productivity in an objective way, which explains partially why compensation often depends only partly, if at all, on output. Hence, where output cannot be measured accurately in an objective fashion, it seems unlikely that employees would be motivated solely by performance-related compensation to increase productivity. Instead, they may be more motivated to give the impression of productivity or engage in other political behaviour to ensure higher compensation (cf. Sparrow, Chapter 10).

In some work, individual output is not so difficult to measure. Nevertheless, even in such work, a close link between the output of the employees and the compensation received is not often observed in reality (e.g. journalists, researchers, software developers). One explanation is that output is subject to external factors that are not under the employees' control. In such work then, a performance-related method of pay is neither always viable nor acceptable to the employees, since employees are not willing to accept the additional uncertainty related to performance-related compensation (see Milgrom and Roberts, 1992). For example, the output of journalists may be easily measured based on the number of articles. However, some journalists may seem to be much more productive when measured based on the number of articles just because of sudden interest in a topic (e.g. war). Many journalists are therefore less willing to accept a job that offers compensation fully based on the number of articles. So it seems that the difficulty of observing the output of the employee, and the fact that output depends often on unknown external factors, makes the usual recommendation to use output-orientated performance measures and performance-related compensation for teleworking highly problematic for many jobs. When performance-related compensation is not an option, managers must rely on additional (costly) forms of monitoring to avoid employees underperforming, for example by engaging in a series of performance review meetings (see earlier). This view is supported by Huws (1993), who identifies two polar extremes of distance management: teleworkers who are paid by results and who do not meet the managers regularly (about 20 per cent of the teleworkers in her sample) and teleworkers who are paid on a regular wage or time basis, and for whom regular meetings are an essential instrument of management.

Differences in ability of teleworkers

In most professions, the productivity of employees depends to a certain extent on the natural ability of employees. Therefore, when recruiting employees, screening of applicants is an important task. On the other hand, when employees do not perform as well as thought during recruitment, employees may be laid off. Clearly, since managers have difficulty observing the behaviour of teleworkers, the chances of detecting underperforming teleworkers are largely reduced. Managers may then consider putting more effort into the screening process, to minimize the risk of hiring underperforming teleworkers (see also Billsberry, Chapter 5 and Omari and Standen, Chapter 12).

Job tenure

Employees differ in the extent to which they expect to stay with an organization. Some employees expect to stay for a short period, while others see their job as more permanent. In addition, in some organizations, job turnover is much higher than in other organizations. It may be argued that expected job tenure is of extreme importance to managers and employees, particularly when employees' behaviour is difficult to observe and when it takes considerable time before sufficient information on the output of employees can be gathered. Employees will realize that the longer they expect to remain with the organization, the more information will be available on their productivity. Hence, the expectation to stay longer with the organization may motivate employees to work harder to avoid being fired or to receive promotion in the future. In addition, the longer that employees expect to stay with the organization, the more they will lose when caught shirking/underperforming. Hence, again, the expectation to stay longer with the organization may motivate employees to put more effort into the production process. To the extent that teleworkers' behaviour is not immediately observable and it is likely to take some time to gain the necessary information to make judgements about their productivity, one might expect organizations to be unwilling to hire teleworkers for short periods. Indeed, van Ommeren (1998) found that the proportion of teleworkers in organizations with higher average turnover is considerably lower than the proportion of teleworkers in organizations with lower average turnover.

More compensation

While employees might have an expectation of remaining for a considerable period with a certain employer, it may not be sufficient to motivate them if they do not lose much when caught underperforming. In addition, when the employer has invested considerably in the employee by means of training, the employer may not be willing to fire underperforming employees. In these situations, the employer may be forced to increase expenditure on monitoring (e.g. by greater use of ICTs or increasing the frequency of meetings), but even this may not be sufficient. By offering employees more compensation than other organizations, employees will lose more when underperforming. Hence, organizations must sometimes be willing to offer teleworkers higher wages than other workers. In a similar way, by offering teleworkers promotion prospects, managers need to rely less on meetings and other monitoring mechanisms, since promotion prospects may reduce the employees' desire to underperform.

Performance appraisal

Teleworkers will receive less informal feedback than other employees, since they are not as closely monitored by their supervisors and have less contact with colleagues. Teleworkers will need, therefore, more information from a formal performance appraisal system to evaluate their performance (Dobbins et al., 1990). When managers carry out performance appraisals of teleworkers, they may choose to use face-to-face contacts or ICTs.

Generally, face-to-face contacts are advisable, since it is more appropriate for a 'correct' interpretation of the appraisal. Teleworking employees will be especially concerned with how their performance is evaluated and which criteria are used to determine performance and compensation. As such, teleworkers are more likely to perceive a combination of behavioural-based and output-based criteria as acceptable than a single performance criterion. In a number of situations, it may be useful for colleagues and customers to contribute to the evaluation of the employee. This arrangement provides the basis for an acceptable principal–agent relationship.

In order to achieve this kind of result, it is necessary first to establish mutually agreed indicators of output and behavioural goals, together with identified factors (as far as one reasonably can) which contribute to or detract from the production of that level of output and the achievement of the behavioural goals. Compensation can then be linked to these outcomes and regular 'mini-appraisals', perhaps using ICTs, can determine the extent to which the agreed compensation should be paid. Appraisals in this form can also be used to identify problems (for example, job design, work/family conflicts, communication difficulties) which should be addressed. At the same time, it is worth considering how compensation might be linked to related factors such as teamwork and organizational learning, and built into the contractual agreement. Apart from the details of the contract, the key to the principal–agent relationship is that there is a clear agreement as to the outputs/goals for which the teleworker will be held to account; how those outputs/goals will be measured; and the rewards/sanctions consequent upon the achievement/non-achievement of the agreed targets.

Conclusion

In this chapter, we have focused on managing and assessing the performance of teleworkers from the perspective offered by principal agent theory. Based on this, we have explained that the usual recommendation of focusing on objective output measures of employees will be useful, but only for a limited number of professions. Other methods to manage the performance of teleworkers are usually needed. One method is to organize regular meetings between managers and employees, which may be useful for many other reasons as detailed elsewhere in this book. Another method is to think more carefully about compensating teleworkers more fully. It is also recommended that the screening and selecting of teleworkers may need more emphasis than usual. Finally, it has been emphasized that teleworking may be less feasible for organizations when job turnover is high.

In Table 15.1, we summarize the recommendations for the performance management of teleworkers, supposing that the employees' on-the-job effort cannot be observed, which is the most plausible assumption for the management of teleworkers. For each of the generic job environments we have identified, there is a recommendation as to the appropriate performance management technique, based on this chapter.

Managing the performance of workers that you cannot see, and therefore over whom you have minimal control, is difficult. Establishing a series of agreed parameters, which frame the working relationship, can help to make that task a little easier.

TABLE 15.1   Performance management of teleworkers

Job environment	Recommendations
Output is costly to observe and variation in output depends strongly on ability	Emphasis on recruitment Regular meetings to discuss difficulties, provide development opportunities
Output can be easily observed and output is only minimally dependent on external factors	Performance-related pay Meetings focused on assessing training and development
Expected job tenure is short and output can be measured	Agreed contract on desired results and performance indicators Performance-related pay
Expected job tenure is long and/or employee has promotion opportunities	Fixed wage Regular meetings to discuss difficulties, provide development opportunities
Expected job tenure is short and output cannot be measured	Do not allow teleworking

References

Barron, J., Black M.D.A. and Loewenstein, M.A. (1987) Employer size: the implications for research, training, capital investment, starting wages, and wage growth. *Journal of Labor Economics*, **5**, 76–89.

Dobbins, G.H., Cardy, R.L. and Platz-Vieno, S. (1990) A contingency approach to appraisal satisfaction: an initial investigation of organizational variables and appraisal characteristics. *Journal of Management*, **16**, 619–32.

Eisenhardt, K.M. (1989) Agency theory: an assessment and review. *Academy of Management Review*, **14**, 57–74.

Gordon, G.E. and Kelly, M.M. (1986) *Teleworking: How to Make it Work for You and Your Company*. Englewood Cliffs, NJ: Prentice Hall.

Huws, U. (1993) *Teleworking in Britain, a Report to the Employment Department*. Research Series no. 18. Sheffield: Employment Department.

IDS (1996) *Teleworking*. Study 616, December, London.

Johnson, S.A. (1998) Teleworking service management: Issues for an integrated framework, in P.J. Jackson and J.M. Van der Wielen (eds) *Teleworking: International Perspectives, From Telecommuting to the Virtual Organization*. London: Routledge.

Milgrom, P. and Roberts, J. (1992) *Economics, Organization and Management*. Englewood Cliffs, NJ: Prentice Hall.

Mokhtarian, P.L. and Salomon, I. (1996) Modelling the choice of teleworking: 3. Identifying the choice set and estimating binary choice models for technology-based alternatives. *Environment and Planning*, **28**, 1877–994.

van Ommeren, J.N. (1998) Telework in Europe, in *Teleworking Environments: Proceedings of the Third International Workshop on Telework*. Turku, Finland.

Chapter 16

Preparing people and organizations for teleworking

Jean Marie Hiltrop

In the past, most organizations grew and developed in a rather *ad hoc* way. Improvements to products or services were often by incremental steps, and new functions and activities were slotted into existing structures, based on capacity or the interest or power of a particular group, rather than improved service or streamlined processes. In recent years, this pattern has changed fundamentally. The pressures of increased competition, resource constraints and the development of advanced technological information systems have led to organizations cutting back their operations; downsizing or outsourcing of non-core activities; and creating lean structures designed to reduce costs and meet changing customer requirements for improved quality and effectiveness. None of these developments will go into reverse. In fact, as we move into the 21st century, we can realistically expect that the pressure to change the culture, purpose and shape of organizations will intensify as the needs for flexibility, competitiveness, innovation, speed and productivity improvements become even greater.

This chapter explores the implications of these developments for future managers and professionals. The key argument is that as organizations are making more use of telework through the use of delayering, outplacement, inter-organizational networking and other changes in organizational structures, the roles and competencies of future managers and professionals will also have to change. There are also implications for human resource management. For example, the new flexible, 'organic' organizations will need new training and development practices which encourage teleworking, and teleworkers themselves will have to live with a large amount of complexity, uncertainty and ambiguity. At the end of the chapter, we make a set of recommendations for accelerating some of the changes and management practices needed to develop and motivate effective teleworkers in organizations.

What are the key issues and challenges?

Teleworking is not a universal phenomenon. In the short term, it may affect only a small group of people and companies in knowledge-intensive industries where innovation determines market leadership, such as consulting, financial services and software development. As McCrimmon puts it:

> Not all organizations will become clones of film production units, where diverse specialists converge for one-off projects, only to disappear into the night once the film is in the can. (1997, p. 17)

In the longer term, however, we can expect organizational structures to become flatter, more complex, more interconnected and more dynamic (see also Lamond, Chapter 3).

Similarly, during the next decades we can realistically expect the following developments to alter fundamentally the shape of organizational structures and create the conditions that lead to implementing and maintaining more telework projects for managers and professionals:

1. *The rules governing successful businesses in the future will be significantly different from those governing successful organizations today.* In *The Transformation Imperative*, Vollmann (1996) argues that the fundamental nature of challenges has altered the competitive environment to such an extent that what once constituted a profile of a winning organization does not necessarily apply any more. As Vollman puts it:

   > All around us we hear the thuds of dinosaur organizations hitting the deck . . . but we need to be alert to notice that a new species has come to life: Its ways are catching hold, and its performance is allowing it to seize the initiative. (1996, p. 11)

2. *The role of the 'boss' is becoming more lateral, with much more focus on people, customers and processes.* In the management literature, the organization of the future is often portrayed as a network of specialists and professionals, with a lean central core servicing various units, alliances and outsourced functions. In this type of company, key roles are those of portfolio specialists, whose value consists in their mastery and experience of the diverse elements essential to the business. At the centre of this development are the sweeping changes in how we define managerial jobs, with the overall purpose of making the organization more adaptable to changing markets. The concept of horizontal process flows has been encouraged by the recent swell of re-engineering efforts. In this concept, the ability of managers to stimulate the creativity, resourcefulness, teamwork, flexibility and innovation of their subordinates is becoming much more important than the ability to command and control the implementation of a precisely defined job. This emphasis on people, processes and customers has wider implications. As Cannon points out:

   > It is not enough for old style bureaucratic managers to add a little mentoring, counselling or walking about to their portfolio of skills.

They will need to regain the trust of the workforce. This might involve a greater involvement in the negative as well as the positive features of corporate life. It is hard to establish trust and credibility on the back of low levels of loyalty, limited technical skills and disproportionate reward systems. (1996, p. 34)

3. *Transactional contracts of employment are becoming the norm in industry.* Many of today's leading management thinkers (e.g. Bridges, 1994; Cappelli, 1999) suggest that job security will continue to decline and people will have to maintain their own employability in the light of downsizing, delayering and reorganization. What is more, there seems to be a growing consensus that the paternalistic 'psychological contract' that governed the relationship between employers and employees in the 1950s and 1960s has ended. Instead, people are being utilized when and where they have needed skills, and can expect to be moved or removed by organizations, as business needs change (see also Sparrow, Chapter 10). It is not surprising, therefore, that many people experience a sense of restlessness inside themselves and in relation to their employers.

These trends are highly consistent with the growing use and importance of teleworking in large professional organizations such as software developers and consulting houses. One possible scenario is that a large group of (professional) teleworkers will become, in a sense, subcontractors to their own companies. Hirsch (1987) has compared this scenario to an employment paradigm which economists call 'free agency'. In this paradigm, people attempt to maximize their personal status and income by selling their individual talents to the highest bidder. Their sense of identity is linked to their profession, rather than to specific companies, teams, offices or functions. They are professionals first, organizational members second.

Implications for managers and professionals

What are the implications of these trends for future managers and professionals? What are the new skill requirements? How can young people prepare themselves for the future? We do not have all the answers, but using current management thinking and reviewing a growing number of books and articles that deal with the future of organizations, some predictions and observations can be made.

More stress

There can be no doubt that non-traditional organizations using teleworking, outsourcing and information technology to improve efficiency and customer responsiveness will be highly demanding places to work. Confronted with the prospect of more freedom, autonomy and responsibility for their own work output, career development and networking, people will have to do their work, think of ways to improve it, and adapt continually to a rapidly changing environment.

To illustrate this point, Table 16.1 lists some of the requirements that an international group of middle managers recently identified as the things that organizations require from their employees today, as well as some of the things that employees demand from their organizations (Hiltrop, 1998). Clearly, the number and variety of items is growing and there is no doubt that these two 'wish lists' – whether actual or anticipated – place immense stress on employers and employees alike. A survey by Demos, an independent think-tank, revealed that 28 per cent of British men work more than 48 hours per week, one in four managers takes work home several times a week, and 60 per cent of men and 45 per cent of women usually or sometimes work Saturdays. Eighty-six per cent of women workers say they never have enough time to get things done. Time off for stress-related illnesses has increased by 500 per cent since the 1950s (Cappelli, 1999). Very often, the net result is increasing dislocation among people, opportunities and the mechanisms to connect them (Nicholson, 1996).

TABLE 16.1   Two wish lists – employers and employees

Employees want	*Employers want*
More …	*More …*
Opportunities	Flexibility
Challenges	Teamwork
Advancement	Availability
Training	Mobility
Support	Creativity
Freedom	Productivity
Interesting work	Profitability
Money	Entrepreneurship
Autonomy	Leadership
Openness	Visibility
Teamwork	Added value
Consistency	Dedication
Responsibility	Resilience
Recognition	Self-reliance
Free time	Change
Stability	Loyalty
Independence	Innovation
Fun	Hard work
with less …	*with less …*
Control	Security
Pressure	Certainty
Supervision	Advancement
Uncertainty	Time
Complexity	Money
Hierarchy	Staff support

New skills and competencies

Most commentators agree that managers of the future will require a more extensive mix of skills and competencies than their predecessors. For instance, Allred *et al.* (1996) argue that, as more companies adopt some type of network structure, managers need to have not only strong technical, commercial and self-governance skills, but also strong collaborative, partnership and relationship skills.

When conducting our research for *The Accidental Manager: Surviving the Transition from Professional to Manager*, we asked a group of senior managers 'What do you think will be the key features of effective management teams in the future?' (Udall and Hiltrop, 1996). Extrapolating from their responses and experiences, we believe future managers and professionals will need to acquire skills and competencies in the following five areas:

- *Information handling skills.* One of the consequences of the IT revolution has been the massive increase in the amount of information which can now be generated through faxes, modems, e-mail networks and telephone links. The problem is often not what to collect, but what to ignore. Clearly managers and professionals of the future will need to be able to use this new technology to generate, select and digest the information they need.
- *Influencing and negotiating skills.* Effective managers have always needed good influencing and negotiating skills, but teleworking managers and professionals will find themselves relying on these skills more and more as a central way of getting things done as relationships with customers, colleagues, subordinates and suppliers are becoming more complex, resources are becoming scarcer, and information, responsibility and authority are decentralized.
- *Teamworking and communication skills.* Increasingly managers and professionals have to rely on their co-workers and trust them to function to quality assured standards with minimal support and supervision. This requires good communication skills to enable performance, provide technical and social support, and at the same time promote teamwork and facilitate change. This also has implications for the development of new leadership styles and organizational cultures (see Standen, Chapter 4 and Lamond, Chapter 11). Many managers say they value, even require teamwork and participation from their co-workers, while at the same time they discourage sharing of resources and information and do not tolerate criticism.
- *Change management skills.* Clearly, managing change has been a key feature of successful management for some time. However, the traditional approach to change, in which the manager acts as the captain of a ship sailing through calm seas, seeing a storm, successfully navigating through it and then returning to calm waters again, no longer holds true. One senior manager described his role as being 'more like white water rafting, than sailing calm seas'. In future, the result of change is highly unlikely to be a new safe and secure island, and future managers will need new skills to cope with rapid and complex change in an increasingly turbulent environment.

- *Visioning and planning skills.* In times of constant change, people need to have a picture of the future, which includes a vision of their contribution to the organization. It may not be possible to support this vision with detailed long-term plans in the same way as in the past, but providing a clear view of a future, together with plans to translate the overall vision into operational reality, is crucial as a point of focus and commitment.

The effective teleworker

What are the implications of these skill requirements for teleworkers? What are the key competencies that are needed by managers and professionals who spend a great deal of time working independently at home and/or on customers' premises? Weiss (1996) argued that most people who seek this type of employment need to develop new and creative abilities. Many of Weiss's themes are captured in Figure 16.1 – a conceptual model of the new career perspectives and requirements (Kiechell, 1994; Hiltrop, 1998). According to this model, the teleworking manager or professional of the future must acquire and show mastery of four key competencies.

1. *Be an expert.* In the (network) organization of the future, managerial roles have been portrayed as those of portfolio specialists, whose work and income come first and foremost from having high expertise in a particular field or subject that is essential to the business. Presumably, getting and retaining high expertise requires the ability to acquire specialist knowledge and having good learning skills adaptability. Hence, the need for a teleworker to be an expert is consistent with Hall's (1996) claim that, in the 21st century, demand in the labour market will shift from those with know-how to those with learn-how; and job security will be replaced by the goal of employability. It follows that teleworkers will need to engage continuously

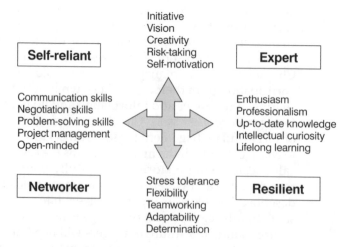

FIGURE 16.1   The future manager profile

in learning and self-development. Their challenge is to keep pace with change and adapt to the evolving needs of the business and customers. Conferences, Internet exchanges and more personal information networks can facilitate this lifelong learning process. When this is done well, teleworkers will have the opportunity to maximize their talents and the result is increased professionalism.

2. *Be a good networker.* Although not all companies will adopt the network structure, even managers who do not become teleworkers increasingly find themselves either directly or indirectly interacting with other functions, cultures and professionals on a global scale. This implies that every manager or professional needs to develop the ability to communicate effectively with a wide diversity of experts and collaborate with multidisciplinary groups of people. Teleworkers certainly need to acquire extensive cross-functional experience. As Allred *et al.* (1996, p. 24) put it:

> Cellular organizations will require most of their staff to be adept project managers because this is the form that much future work will take. Managers will need a basic understanding of other functions' paradigms and approaches so that multidisciplinary resources can be quickly assembled and utilised.

3. *Be self-reliant.* The changing psychological contract is one widespread indication of the pressing need for teleworkers to be competent at managing themselves (see Sparrow, Chapter 10). In network organizations where most of the non-core work is done by subcontractors, homeworkers and self-employed service providers, the paternalism that existed in the 1950s and 1960s has gone, so that the majority of people simply cannot rely on someone else to take responsibility for their career and income. In the most flexible organizational forms, teleworkers will have no job security. This means, of course, that many people will have to disengage from the psychological benefits that a secure job provides and learn how to manage their own business. Without a company and boss determining when and where to perform their work, they will have to learn how to manage their time, including time spent with their families.

4. *Be resilient.* In a turbulent environment, people who prefer stability and/or linear careers are liable to become the new losers (Brousseau *et al.*, 1996). Therefore, what teleworkers need (in addition to the technical and social skills needed to become an expert, networker and self-reliant) is the ability to live with high levels of uncertainty, to bend and not break and to bounce back quickly from failure and disappointment. In other words, the move to teleworking will require managers and professionals, among other things, to become highly 'resilient' – a state of mind they can achieve by developing the following three characteristics:
   - *Feeling in control* of one's life, rather than powerless to influence external, capricious, or even malicious forces. Resilient people tend to interpret stressful situations positively and optimistically and they respond to change constructively. They take responsibility for their actions and feel they are in charge of their own destinies.

- *Feeling committed* to and involved in what one is doing, rather than alienated from one's work and other individuals. Resilient people not only feel that they choose what they do, but strongly believe in the importance of what they do.
- *Feeling challenged* by new experiences rather than viewing change as a threat to security and comfort. Typically resilient people prefer change to stability and view challenging experiences as a necessary step toward learning. They tend to have high tolerance for uncertainty and perform best under stress. As a result, their propensity to illness and emotional dysfunction under stressful conditions is considerably below the norm. (See also Maddi and Kobasa, 1984.)

No doubt some people are better equipped to cope with this challenge than others. We can assume that personality traits and professional backgrounds (education, career history, international experience, etc.) will play an important role in determining an individual's level of resilience. For this reason, some career counsellors advise people who have been displaced from traditional organizations to avoid seeking a specific job in a particular industry, but instead learn to be flexible enough to take advantage of whatever opportunities come along (Allred *et al.*, 1996).

Acquiring the new competencies

Clearly, according to this model, managers and professionals who spend a great deal of time outside the traditional organizational locations (such as consultants, salespeople, international project managers and independent service providers) have to develop a much wider and deeper range of skills and competencies than their colleagues in more traditional jobs and organizations. For many people, the move from traditional manager or professional to teleworker *and* networker will not be easy, as it will require the unlearning of various dysfunctional behaviours. For some people, the move will require them not only to develop a broader and deeper range of competencies, but also to challenge the underlying assumptions, which they have been using for a long time to manage themselves and others. As Noer (1997, p. 61) puts it:

> In times of transition, downsizing, and restructuring, organizations drop some heavy rocks in our packs ... Those with overwhelmed and entrenched response patterns have a particularly difficult time. The rocks they must bear are called anger, fear, guilt, depression, and anxiety – and they are exceptionally heavy!

The swamp metaphor

How can managers and professionals survive the transition from traditional roles and functions to those of teleworker? What advice can we give to those who choose or need to change their employment relationship from full-time on-site employee to external off-site service provider? A recent study by Quick *et al.* (1990) of executive performance under stress suggests that there are four strategies that managers and professionals can use to cope with their rapidly changing environment. They are:

- *Intellectual curiosity.* Being intellectually curious expands a person's understanding of the world, providing perspective as well as knowledge for problem solving.
- *Be physically active.* People who are physically active dissipate stress-induced energy while at the same time developing a stronger, more efficient cardiovascular system.
- *Balance work with non-work.* People who balance work with non-work activities place their work in a larger, broader context of life that gives them perspective and reduces psychological dependence.
- *Seek social support.* Supportive relationships provide people with the means to meet a variety of their emotional, informational and evaluative needs, essential to healthy functioning.

Although using these strategies can be useful to help you cope with the transition from traditional employee to teleworker, doing so will not eliminate the uncertainty and stress you experience from your new role. On the contrary, sustaining a vision while not being certain of how you will achieve it, processing vast quantities of information, fostering creativity and learning, negotiating with customers and suppliers, and, at the same time, relying on teams of co-workers to deliver high-quality products and services are all potentially threatening to one's personal sense of security and well-being. In other words, stress will remain a necessary component of telework due to the nature of the new organization and work environment.

Consider, therefore, the use of the swamp metaphor. In our workshops with managers and professionals from both public and sector organizations, Sheila Udall and I have been using this metaphor to help people cope with major transitions in their work and personal life (Udall and Hiltrop, 1996). The swamp metaphor is one of leaving a secure place, an island, and crossing water to a new island, hoping that it offers the same kind of security, but not really being too sure what to expect. In order to cross a swamp you need to be able to swim through the 'watery places', have lifelines to pull you through, or stepping stones to lift you from the 'boggy bits'. Similarly, in order to be an effective manager you need the relevant skills (*like swimming*), help and support (*lifelines*) to perform well. In the swamp, irritators and challenges are all around. The irritators (in the form of *flies* and *mosquitoes*) include events and people who distract you from your daily tasks and roles. The *alligators* are the pressures and challenges of growing competition, government regulations and social policy initiatives, senior management decisions, increasingly sophisticated technology and the changing attitudes and expectations of staff, bosses, customers and suppliers.

Hence, given the overall mix of managerial competencies required by effective teleworkers, many managers may feel they are trying to cross a swamp. However, adapting to change, like crossing a swamp, is not always smooth. It is almost inevitable that you will make mistakes (you may fall into the swamp); there will be setbacks (you get stuck in the mud); and there may be discomfort (you get your feet wet). For these reasons, managers who are crossing the swamp may benefit from such lifelines as mentoring, coaching and feedback, before reaching the new firm ground and feeling confident and competent again in their new role.

In future the result of change is unlikely to be a new safe and secure island, and managers will need to take 'calculated' risks to cope with rapid and complex change in an increasingly turbulent environment. The new island, therefore, will have limited 'firm ground' and its foundations will be under constant threat of erosion.

Implications for human resource management

The implications for HRM are both profound and far-reaching. For instance, although there will continue to be places for all types of employment relationships (from the traditional manager/professional to the more recent teleworker), we can expect that in most industries only those companies adopting a variety of employment systems and practices will survive the dawn of the flexible, process-orientated organization.

Moreover, with the projection of middle-aged employees comprising a larger part of the workforce in most industrialized countries, and with work becoming more unstable and demanding, organizations have good reason to be interested in preparing people for the future. Already there are signs that the number of individuals who experience career entrenchment is increasing dramatically (Carson and Carson, 1997). A survey of over a thousand middle-aged men in managerial and professional positions found that five out of every six respondents endured a period of severe frustration and trauma which began in their early 30s. Work performance, emotional stability and physical health were seriously affected (Sonnenfeld, 1989). Some people would like to change careers, but wanting to change, of course, is not the same as doing it. According to Carson and Carson (1997), many organizations are burdened with workers who want to jump ship, but who stay firmly on board grasping for long-term security in the face of widespread job cuts, yet without displaying commitment to their organizations. Candidates for second careers tend to be in their mid-40s and report a perceived discrepancy between personal aspirations and current opportunities for achievement and promotion. This group is likely become larger as the opportunity for advancement decreases, resulting in major career frustration and entrenchment among middle managers.

So how can organizations help people prepare for teleworking? What are the implications for the management of people? Once again, we do not have all the answers, but a number of suggestions can be made to accelerate some of the changes needed to help operationalize successful teleworking in large organizations today.

Replace outdated training and development practices

In a turbulent and ever-changing business world, replacing the traditional training and development programmes that have supplied deep hierarchical structures with a steady diet of 'qualified' people for many decades is quickly becoming a necessity (see Salmon *et al.*, Chapter 14). As Morgan puts it:

> More than ever the world is in flux. And organizations and their managers must recognise the necessity of developing the mindsets, skills and abilities that will allow them to cope with this flux. (1988, p. 15)

Increasingly, organizations will need to find systems and practices that promote entrepreneurship and learning (see Tregaskis and Daniels, Chapter 13). Managers and professionals, in turn, will have to learn how to use the vast amounts of data which have become available with the information technology revolution, and learn to live with the complexity and ambiguity created by the competitive forces buffeting organizations today.

Build new skills through innovative 'practice fields'

In *The Paradox Principles*, Cannon (1996) emphasizes the need to give managers and employees more opportunities to practise the skills that are needed to perform well in the emerging business environment. He argues that classroom teaching and role-playing does not qualify: it is seldom realistic or relevant. He therefore suggests that organizations create 'practice fields' that let managers and employees hone their skills and gain experience under realistic but risk-free conditions. The Productivity Enhancement Programme at Bell Labs is a useful example. According to Cannon (1996), the company asked a number of its star engineers to develop an expert model. The result was a set of nine prioritized work strategies that the engineers believed other employees could master. Training sessions to pass on these strategies occur in the normal workday. Productivity increases in both star and average performers have been striking, from a 10 per cent increase immediately after the sessions to 25 per cent after a full year. Motorola has reported similar productivity gains from a similar programme. However, the most important 'product' of this approach is managers who understand how to create a learning environment for those around them (Cannon, 1996).

These observations are supported by the findings of recent studies that explored the changing educational demands of employers. For instance, Rajan (1997) argues for what he calls a 'flexible mindset' to take account of the changing demands of employers and the disappearance of paternalism and formal career structures in many organizations. In such a mindset, he states, the employee begins to treat the employer as a customer and the work becomes a product. Qualities such as negotiation and selling become important in the preparation and discussion of a work assignment. There is a close resemblance between these findings and those of Kotter (1996), who tracked the careers of 115 Harvard MBA graduates from the class of 1974. Kotter found that more than one-third of the graduates had been dismissed from a job or had been made redundant at least once by 1992. Many had moved to smaller businesses and some had set up their own companies. In fact, by 1992 the proportion of graduates in large and medium-sized enterprises had decreased from 71 per cent to 38 per cent. Like Rajan in the UK, Kotter concludes that the US education system must wake up to the changing nature of careers and invest greater resources into promoting interpersonal, leadership and teamworking skills. Students must be encouraged, he says, to develop a competitive drive and desire for lifelong learning.

Facilitate career mobility and change

Some companies are already adopting new HR practices to increase job mobility between and within their organizations. Cable & Wireless, for example, has set up what it calls career action centres to help people make inter-company moves and to encourage a 'contract mentality' where employees think of their work in terms of a series of projects rather than as a lifelong career (Donkin, 1997). Furthermore, to facilitate the transition from traditional roles to teleworking, organizations can take a number of initiatives, including the following (Carson and Carson, 1997):

- providing ongoing career counselling, mentoring and outplacement assistance to all employees, not just those who are made redundant;
- offering training, time off and financial help to those who want to attend courses to improve their skills and competence, even if these skills are not highly organizational or career specific;
- allowing employees to make career changes within the organization, rather than forcing them to stay within their (functional) career ladder;
- encouraging employees to think about career planning issues and not making them feel guilty or disloyal as they explore new career options;
- allowing employees who wish to change careers to leave in good standing and to return if they do not succeed;
- providing traditional benefits to teleworkers such as portable pension plans, health plans and other accumulated forms of compensation.

Each of these methods is aimed at reducing the progression of career entrenchment and at encouraging people to take more responsibility for their self-development and career planning (Hiltrop, 1998). Some of these initiatives may result in some turnover, as a number of individuals may recognize the need to abandon their current occupational paths and explore new ones. However, as we enter the 21st century, the cost of turnover is likely to be of less concern than the tribulations of career stagnation and entrenchment.

Promote individual growth and development through real teamwork

Almost daily, teleworkers face complex situations in which they must rely on others to get their work done. In some organizations, such as consulting houses and public aid organizations (e.g. the Red Cross, Médecins Sans Frontières, Oxfam), teleworkers depend on their peers and subordinates for their rewards, recognition, appraisal and training. Moreover, employees in the 21st century may periodically have to backtrack their own careers, moving from teleworker back to on-site trainee as they are required to develop new competencies. Cianni and Wnuck (1997) suggest that adaptation to these changes and movement into unfamiliar roles may take place more smoothly within a supportive team environment, where all team members recognize the importance of others' career development. As organizations evolve to become more flexible, a compelling case can then be made for team-oriented career development systems. In any case, the challenges of the 21st century call for innovative solutions that complement the existing methods of performance evaluation, compensation and training.

Table 16.2 gives examples of how some companies are adapting to the new realities.

TABLE 16.2   Managing teleworkers in virtual teams: some company examples

1. **Digital Equipment** tries to recruit employees with good communication skills, and those who are able to establish themselves in 'virtual teams' with a minimum of direction from above. Members of a virtual team must be well educated and require above-average networking skills.
2. **Arco Chemical Europe** has developed training activities to encourage team-building among employees who may otherwise rarely meet one another. The company advises its teleworkers to set aside a reasonable amount of time for video-conferences and, if possible, to move to a different room from the one they normally work in.
3. **The British Council**, which employs 6000 people in 109 countries, spent more than £250,000 on a series of week-long workshops in 1996, followed by two-day roadshows for employees in each country. The objective was to weld together people who will not meet again in the flesh for up to two years – if at all.
4. **British Telecom** uses virtual teams spread over a number of sites in the UK and overseas, many of whom work in different time zones. Most team members are young. As the Head of Research explains: 'The people we employ tend to be 25 to 27 years old. They are used to teamworking from their school days and they don't come with this stupid management culture that says information is power.'
5. **IBM and Lotus Institute** have produced two programmes – TeamRoom and WorkRoom – designed to enable virtual teams to work together. As one employee says 'If you have 10 people located in 10 different places and they are not all sure that they know what they're doing, chaos breaks out. It is critical that they establish a relationship and trust each other.'
6. **Other organizations** have changed their human resource systems to adapt to the new realities. Allied Signal, Andersen Consulting, Chevron and Lotus Development, among others, have already built databases showing which people have what knowledge and skills, using them to create a virtual marketplace where resource-providers and project managers shop for talent.

Give HR managers a pivotal role in implementing the new agenda

Preparing people for teleworking requires systems and procedures to align individual and organizational objectives; enable communication amongst workers; develop them effectively; asses their potential and performance; give them feedback; and help them plan and manage their careers. Each of these activities has traditionally been the responsibility of the HR department. Despite all the talk about strategic human resource management, however, most HR managers remain stuck in their administrative roles processing complaints and paperwork. Indeed, one of the most worrying findings in studies of HRM is how few HR managers put themselves at the forefront of developing human talent in their companies. For instance, when asked about the two highest priorities of their department, only one out of every three HR managers in the Laborforce 2000 survey gave top priority to improving the quality of their company's workforce or rated employee training and management development as central thrusts of their function (Lawler *et al.*, 1993). What is more, 25 per cent of the HR managers reported that either they have no major responsibility for meeting their company's strategic objectives, or they simply are not sure where they fit in. The authors concluded, therefore, that very few human resource departments are true partners with line managers in running the business.

Conclusion

There is no doubt that teleworkers need a very different set of skills and competencies than their colleagues in more traditional roles and functions. For some people the picture painted in this chapter might be unappealing, frightening or simply 'not acceptable'. They may prefer some of the on-site job alternatives that are offered by large organizations, get stuck in their current job or leave for another company. But even if the challenges and benefits of teleworking are unappealing to some people, they may not have much choice.

Moreover, it can be argued that teleworking offers a structured approach to competence-based development of employees. When done well, it can provide them with a number of benefits, including access to professional networks, the ability to achieve a better balance between home and work and the opportunity to plan work and development activities independent of a line manager, who will be more likely to focus on performance. Overall, this suggests that: (1) a teleworking scheme can be an effective approach to the development of staff; and (2) being a teleworker can provide a unique career and learning opportunity for managerial and professional staff. On the other hand, the author's own experience with helping organizations to implement teleworking suggests that there are a number of caveats that need to be raised as well. These include the following:

1. *Teleworkers' roles and responsibilities must be clarified and agreed in advance.* The respective roles of teleworkers and on-site employees should be made clear to everyone, and the teleworker's role specification should be challenging and important enough to give the teleworker credibility and authority with other workers. For example, in consulting, on-site employees are more concerned with enabling organizational performance through effective research and development, while the consultant's role is more focused on operational issues, customer service delivery and market share building. Clearly these roles are not mutually exclusive. Most consultants take their own responsibility for research and development very seriously but they may have less time, or different skills, to do these tasks. The roles can and should be complementary, but equally the boundary between them needs to be openly discussed and agreed.

2. *Senior managers need to understand and be committed to the scheme.* The attitude of senior managers to any scheme has a significant effect down the line, through line managers to teleworkers themselves. If senior managers are not supportive, it can easily affect the level of commitment of traditional line managers and generate additional issues for the teleworker. This is particularly true in organizations where the teleworking scheme is initiated and/or orchestrated by the human resource department. In such cases, it may not be enough to keep line managers informed in writing about the teleworking scheme, as some of them may need to be actively included in dialogue to understand, engage in and give their full commitment to the success of the scheme.

3. *The teleworking scheme needs to fit into a broader vision and strategy.* Teleworking cannot work in a vacuum. The vision of the senior management team is central to the success of alternative approaches to working and the teleworking scheme needs to be aligned with the various management initiatives and practices that are designed to promote organizational flexibility and customer responsiveness. These may include the use of flexitime, annual hours, performance-related pay, process re-engineering and supply chain management.

4. *Changing the traditional culture and structure to make teleworking work takes time.* Changing managerial mindsets from traditional working arrangements to teleworking and self-reliance is unlikely to be accomplished in a short period of time. It is a learning process in itself and the usual process of 'Unfreezing–Change–Refreezing' will take time to apply. People do not adjust to change instantly (especially if it is not 'self-selected') and, to some extent, the specific forms of teleworking that work best for a business unit or organization need to be developed incrementally in the light of feedback from those who practise it. However, once teleworking is embedded into the organization's structure, culture and systems, becoming a teleworker can provide a unique opportunity for continuous professional development. When implemented well, it may give a real sense of accomplishment to people who may otherwise become stuck in one role and at one level in the organization.

Implicit in these recommendations are lessons not just for individuals but for large organizations. As Donkin (1997) points out, if talented people are increasingly drawn to smaller enterprises where they are receiving more job satisfaction and more income than most of those in traditional large organizations, big companies must wake up to the implications of this trend for employee recruitment and development. Perhaps they need to become more proactive and creative in creating new or better opportunities for young and talented people to mobilize their enthusiasm and potential. Preparing people for the future, therefore, goes much further than providing the future managers and professionals with the skills and competencies needed to become teleworkers and grow or maintain the businesses set up by earlier generations of entrepreneurs.

References

Allred, B., Snow, C. and Miles, R. (1996) Characteristics of managerial careers in the 21st century. *Academy of Management Executive*, **10**, Special issue, 17–27.

Bridges, W. (1994) *Job Shift*. Reading: Addison-Wesley.

Brousseau, K., Driver, M., Eneroth, K. and Larsson, R. (1996) Career pandemonium: realigning organizations and individuals. *Academy of Management Executive*, **10**, Special issue, 52–66.

Cannon, T. (1996) *Welcome to the Revolution*. London: Pitman Publishing.

Cappelli, P. (1999) *The New Deal at Work: Managing the Market-Driven Workforce*. Boston: Harvard Business School Press.

Carson, K. and Carson, P. (1997) Career entrenchment: a quiet march toward occupational death? *Academy of Management Executive*, **11**, February, 62–75.

Cianni, M. and Wnuck, D. (1997) Individual growth and team enhancement: moving toward a new model of career development. *Academy of Management Executive*, **11**, February, 105–15.

Donkin, R. (1997) Lessons in high performance. *Financial Times*, Wednesday, 13 August.

Hall, D. (1996) Protean career of the 21st century. *Academy of Management Executive*, **10**, Special issue, 8–16.

Hiltrop, J.M. (1998) Preparing people for the future: the next agenda for HRM. *European Management Journal*, **16**, 70–8.

Hirsch, P. (1987) *Pack Your Own Parachute*. Reading: Addison-Wesley.

Kiechell, W. (1994) A manager's career in the new economy. *Fortune*, 4 April.

Kotter, J. (1996) *The New Rules*. Boston: Simon and Schuster.

Lawler, E., Cohen, S. and Lei Chang (1993) Strategic human resource management. In P.H. Mirvis (ed.) *Building the Competitive Workforce*. New York: Wiley.

Maddi, S.R. and Kobasa, S.C. (1984) *The Hardy Executive: Health Under Stress*. Homewood, Illinois: Dow-Jones Irvin.

McCrimmon, M. (1997). Choices in the careers cafeteria, *Human Resources*, May–June, 17.

Morgan, G. (1988) *Riding the Waves of Change*. San Francisco: Jossey-Bass.

Nicholson, N. (1996) Career systems in crisis: change and opportunity in the information age. *Academy of Management Executive*, **10**, Special issue, 40–51.

Noer, D. (1997) *Breaking Free: A Prescription for Personal and Organizational Change*. San Francisco: Jossey-Bass.

Quick, J., Nelson, D. and Quick, J (1990) *Stress and Challenge at the Top: The Paradox of the Successful Executive*. New York: Wiley.

Rajan A. (1997) *Tomorrow's People.* Turnbridge Wells: Create.

Sonnenfeld, J. (1989) Dealing with the ageing work force. In R. Levinson (ed.) *Designing and Managing Your Career.* Boston: Harvard University Press.

Udall, S. and Hiltrop, J. (1996) *The Accidental Manager: Surviving the Transition from Professional to Manager.* London: Prentice Hall.

Vollmann, T. (1996) *The Transformation Imperative.* Boston: Harvard University Press.

Weiss, J. (1996) *Organizational Behavior and Change.* New York: West Publishing Company.

Chapter 17

Prospects and perspectives

Kevin Daniels, David Lamond and Peter Standen

How telework will evolve in the future is the subject of great speculation in the media and the academic press. In the last chapter Hiltrop reminds us that the rapidly changing management environment means that skills and competencies that were sufficient in the past are no longer adequate, and suggests that teleworkers in particular will need a much broader set of abilities. Hiltrop also pointed to a number of a grim prospects facing teleworkers and their managers – recalling the warnings of Sparrow earlier (Chapter 10) that teleworking can be in danger of degenerating into a low-trust form of work, riddled with little more than impression management. Indeed, as van Ommeren (Chapter 15) illustrates, there might be ways of managing performance in such low-trust environments. However, as industries become more knowledge intensive and telework becomes more central to business processes, there are ways to prevent the worst that the future might have to offer, or at least to buffer organizations and teleworkers against it. Indeed, many of the contributions to this book have outlined ways in which this can be achieved through effective line management, supported and directed by effective human resource management in making telework successful for all parties.

Effective management does not mean a narrow focus on productivity. One theme that emerges from the contributions is that the usual adage of managing teleworkers by outputs is often not a sensible option. As van Ommeren illustrates, not only is this often very difficult to achieve, even from a hard-nosed performance management perspective, but it is not always desirable either. Neither is relying purely on developments in technology to improve productivity and coordination. To this we might add Moon and Stanworth's (1997) call for an ethical approach to managing teleworkers, so that telework is *not* used to worsen terms and conditions, to weaken or eliminate trade union representation or to replace childcare facilities. It then becomes apparent that, instead of simply managing the outputs of teleworkers or the teleworking process, the most appropriate approach is to manage the outputs, the process *and* the context of teleworking. This approach is illustrated in Figure 17.1.

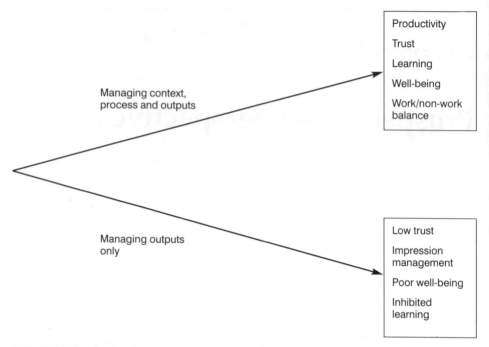

FIGURE 17.1   Approaches to managing telework: contexts, processes and outputs

As illustrated throughout the book, such an approach can help address Moon and Stanworth's (1997) concerns and help against the uncertainties and problems highlighted by Hiltrop and Sparrow. Placing greater emphasis on the management of teleworkers can have benefits for both organizations and teleworkers. Daniels (Chapter 8) and Standen (Chapter 9) have highlighted approaches that can help promote teleworkers' well-being and maintain a healthy balance between work and non-work activities. At the group and organizational level, Harper (Chapter 6) and Salmon *et al.* (Chapter 14) illustrate quite powerfully how paying attention to processes can help technologically driven innovations enhance communication and the implementation of training and development programmes. To these cases, Tregaskis and Daniels (Chapter 13) highlight how paying attention to context and process can enhance organizational learning capability, through proper use of technology and creation of the right social environment.

Within all this, as Lamond (Chapter 11) illustrates in his chapter on management style, managers must make an effort to build the supportive environments, organizational cultures and trust needed to ensure the best results from teleworking. At the same time, managers need to be aware that without careful attention, teleworking can sink into the low-trust environment of which Sparrow warns us. We would argue strongly that, in an era when the psychological contract is increasingly problematic as a concept that underpins the employer–employee relationship, managers' ability to develop trust in these conditions becomes critical. Equally critical is the notion of 'authenticity'.

Reichers *et al.* (1997) talk about the need to understand and manage employee cynicism during organizational change. In the same way, managers need to understand and manage the cynicism of employees as they cast a wary eye over the introduction of teleworking and/or the complementary introduction of new ways of managing. Unless managers are authentic in their relations with their employees, a 'healthy' level of cynicism will persist.

Yet, managers can be helped to build trust and authenticity by carefully crafting career and compensation systems suitable to the particular contexts of teleworkers. As van Ommeren argues, such systems could begin to improve performance even before trust is fully developed. So too, selection systems can be developed to assist managers in building the best environments. As argued by Billsberry (Chapter 5), Lamond (Chapter 7) and Omari and Standen (Chapter 12), selection should proceed on the basis of matching the applicant to the form of teleworking to be undertaken – on the basis of alignment with organizational values, personality, competencies and match with the non-work environment. Tregaskis and Daniels suggest that, where teams need to be assembled rapidly, for instance in virtual project teams spanning several organizations, electronic archives could be used to assemble teams rapidly by identifying individuals with the right profiles for the task at hand (Townsend *et al.*, 1998; see also De Fillippi and Arthur, 1998). Indeed, the systemic approach to selection outlined by Omari and Standen illustrates how managers and human resource management systems need to be sensitive to both the process of teleworking and the strategic and social contexts of organizations.

Teleworking is likely to be successful where teleworking forms part of an integrated human resource management system that supports organizational strategy. As highlighted in the early chapters of Tregaskis (Chapter 2), Lamond (Chapter 3) and Standen (Chapter 4), this means implementing telework programmes that are compatible with organizational strategies, structures and cultures, and which are suited to prevailing economic and social conditions. Certainly, analysis of the organization and its environment is important for deciding whether teleworking is consonant with current conditions, or whether organizational structures, cultures and processes need to be modified to suit teleworking practices. Later chapters in the book have illustrated how technology management, socialization processes, job design, psychological contracting and career management, selection systems, training and development practices and performance management can all ensure a match between teleworking practices and the macro-economic, organizational, social and psychological environments. However, neither the pushes and pulls on effective teleworking nor economic environments stand still. Further, as noted by Hamel and Prahalad (1993), effective organizational performance comes not just from fitting the environment, but by developing and using organizational resources in new and more effective ways. For these reasons, human resource management practices should not just ensure that teleworking fits its niche in the organization, but that the possibilities of teleworking are explored and developed. Indeed, it is important more generally that the human resource management be genuinely strategic and contribute to the development of corporate strategy rather than merely reflect it.

We hope this book encourages managers to explore the possibilities of tele-working, keeping in mind the broader issues of processes and context as well as productivity or efficiency gains. The opening chapter presents an overarching framework showing how the various elements of teleworking and human resource management can fit together to maximize the benefits for organizations and individuals. Throughout the book, contributors have developed detailed analyses and models of these elements, and noted how they differ for the various forms of telework. What has emerged in this book is that there is no 'one best way' of managing teleworkers, not least because there are many different forms of teleworking. Rather, each situation presents a unique set of circumstances that requires a unique approach to its management. Notwithstanding, these analyses and models can enable managers to reflect on insights and prescriptions offered here, elsewhere and on their own experiences, and to develop their own evolving models of best practice for their own contexts.

References

DeFillippi, R.J. and Arthur, M.B. (1998) Paradox in project-based enterprise: the case of film making, *California Management Review*, **40**, 125–39.

Hamel, G. and Prahalad, C.K. (1993) Strategy as stretch and leverage. *Harvard Business Review*, March–April, 75–84.

Moon, C. and Stanworth, C. (1997) Ethical issues in teleworking. *Business Ethics: A European Review*, **6**, 35–45.

Reichers, A.E., Wanous, J.P. and Austin, J.T. (1997) Understanding and managing cynicism about organizational change. *Academy of Management Executive*, **11**, February, 48–58.

Townsend, A.M., DeMarie, S. and Hendrickson, A.R. (1998) Virtual teams: technology and the workplace of the future. *Academy of Management Executive*, **12**, August, 17–29.

Index